Jacque Rupp

The Red Purse

A Story of Grief and Desire

Daylight

20 YEARS

Cofounders: Taj Forer and Michael Itkoff
Creative Director: Ursula Damm
Copy Editor: Gabrielle Fastman

ISBN: 978-1-954119-26-0

Printed by Ofset Yapimevi, Turkey

Daylight Books
E-mail: info@daylightbooks.org
Web: www.daylightbooks.org

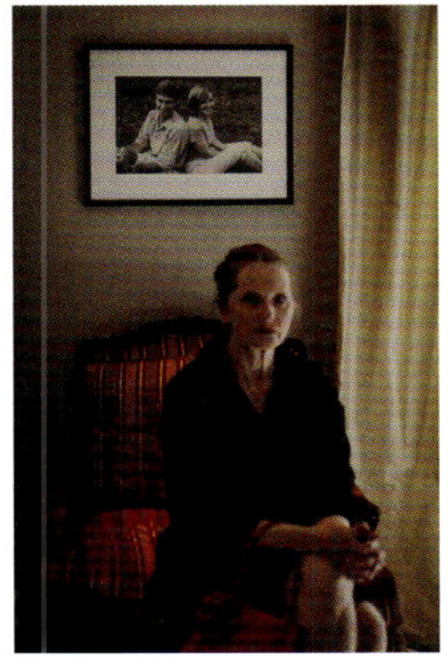

To Edward

The Red Purse

Shortly after he died, I bought a red purse. I knew I needed it, but I didn't know why. For years, the purse sat untouched on my dresser, waiting for me to take up its call.

The Red Purse tells a story of transition, of rebuilding. The project grew from a journey—my journey of navigating through and beyond the darkness and uncertainty of young widowhood.

After my husband passed, I was overcome with grief, with sadness, with fear, but other emotions—confusing, even shameful emotions—soon struck: a rush of femininity, a burst of sexuality, an unexpected exhilaration. Alone with two young boys, I struggled to absorb and understand these disparate, and at times unsettling, feelings and desires.

Coincidentally, my mother also became a widow at a young age. In her day, she had no choice but to shut down, to keep her desires hidden, to stay devoted to her lost husband. By the time my husband passed, though, expectations for widows had eased. While a blessing, this freedom left me in a state of flux, without a set path to follow, without peers or role models to consult.

I had trouble thinking of myself as a widow, unwilling, at first, to join that club. I paused whenever I encountered a "marital status" box on a form, torn between wanting to honor the marriage that was, and knowing that I needed to move on, to create a new identity.

From early in the grieving process, one thing was certain: I did not want to raise my boys under a shroud of loss. I did not want people to pity us. I would, however difficult, press forward, using the confusion, the liminality, as an opportunity to grow.

The red purse stood as a daily reminder: stand tall, be strong, but make room for femininity, for frivolity, for spontaneity.

I started with the easy changes, small actions, focusing first on my environment. I redecorated my home, rearranged furniture, incorporated my own style. But difficult decisions awaited: How would I approach the world as an unmarried woman? I knew I eventually wanted a new partner, a new relationship, a tribute, of course, to my marriage, to what I had lost. But would I be desirable? Was I being disloyal?

I slowly, cautiously, stepped outside of my grief. First, I sought answers—and comfort— from movies, from books, from dreams. I connected with others, those who had overcome obstacles; I shared my hopes and fears with friends and guides. Then, ever so slowly, I ventured out into the world. I explored new places, took spur-of-the-moment trips. I expanded my social circle. Eventually, I dared to flirt, to date.

Rejoining the world did not come easy. When I had fun, guilt ate away at me; when things did not go well, shame prevailed. I felt awkward, unsure. Should I be dating? Could motherhood and sexuality coexist? I alternated between ups and downs, excitement and embarrassment. Confusion reigned—for years—but gradually, I became bolder. I tried out new roles, new personalities, new styles. I experimented with fashion. I felt, at times, like an actress in my own movie, often a film noir—complete with danger, drama, and suspense.

*****

Nearly twenty years have passed, and I have landed, with strength, in a warm and welcoming space, buoyed by acceptance: acceptance of myself and acceptance from others. Grief and loss remain, but they have become silent, almost comforting companions; reminders of a lovely time, of a life well lived.

I now have a long-time partner; my sons are grown and thriving. And I, with awe and wonder, move forward, focused on my passions—my family, my partner, the visual arts—proud of my new life, a vibrant and engaged life, and thankful for the path that brought me here.

After all this time, I still pause at "marital" boxes on forms; there is no word to accurately describe my status. Yes, I am a widow. Yes, I am in a committed relationship. But more importantly, I am a woman redefined, a woman who crossed over a threshold and came out stronger, came out freer, came out more alive.

The Red Purse project is, in the end, not a tale of grief but rather a toast to life, to redefining, to flourishing. *The Red Purse*, a fictionalized account of my story, is meant to inspire, to prompt conversation, to pay tribute to those who have lost, to those who have struggled, and to those who have evolved.

Liminality (from the Latin word limen*, meaning a threshold) is the quality of ambiguity or disorientation that occurs when a person is no longer who they once were and has not yet become someone new and entirely solid.*

—Megan Devine, *It's OK That You're Not OK: Meeting Grief and Loss in a Culture That Doesn't Understand*

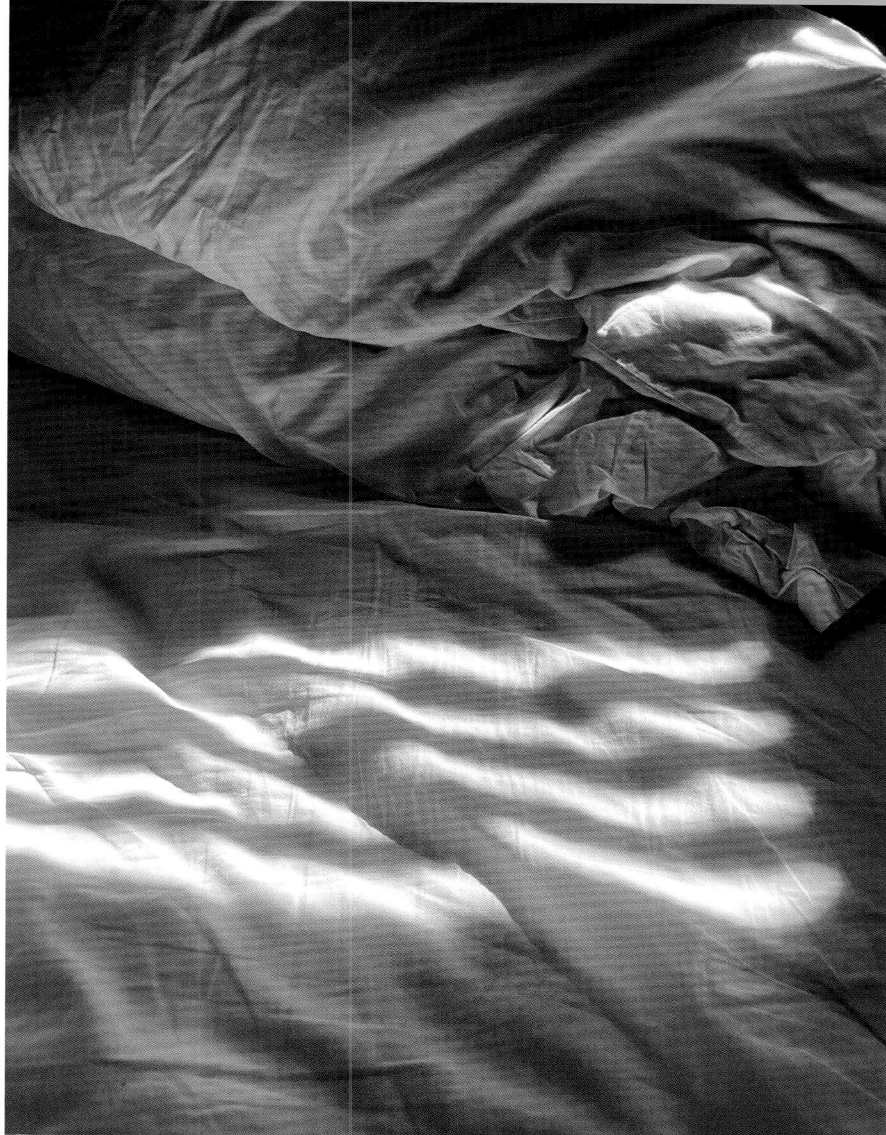

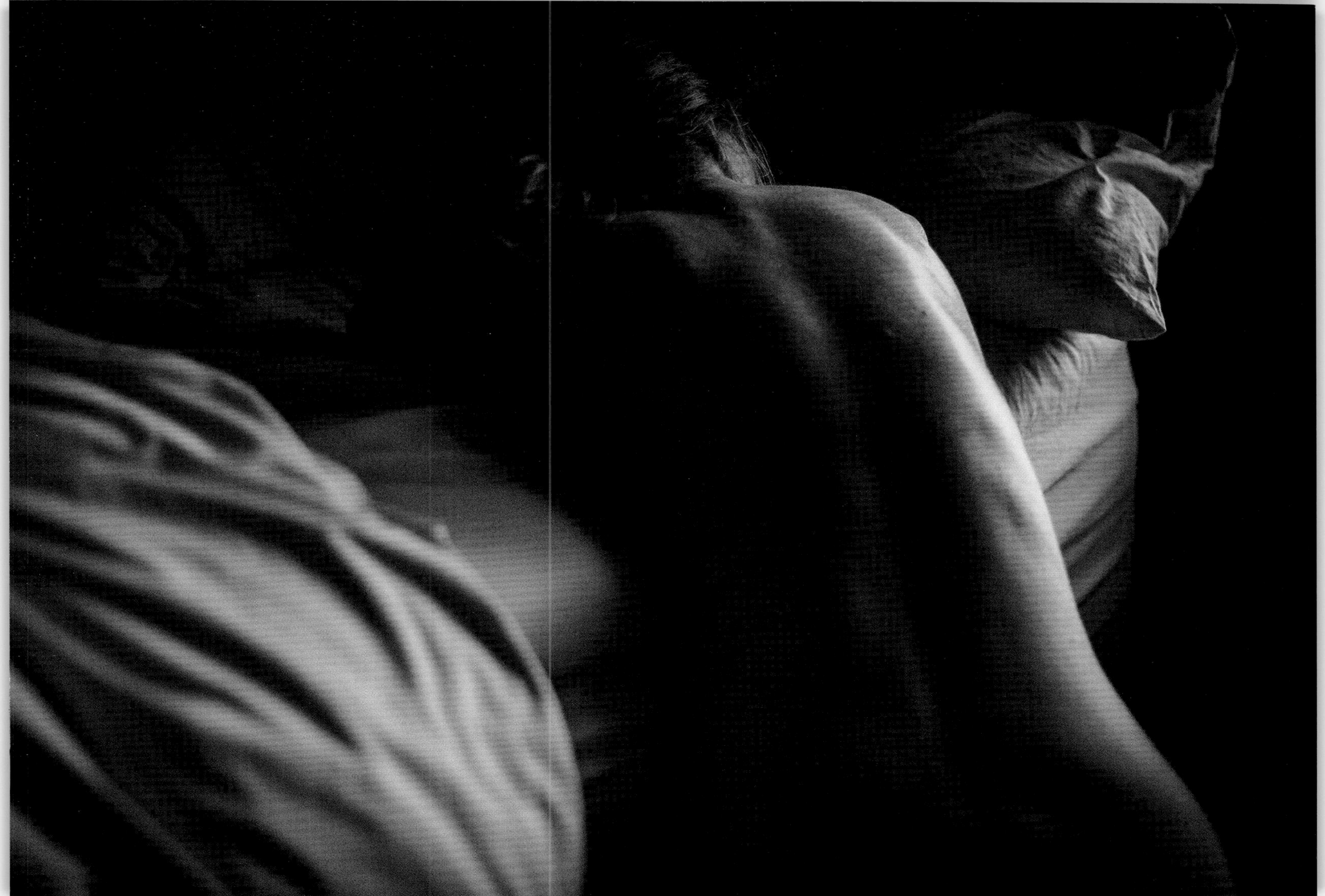

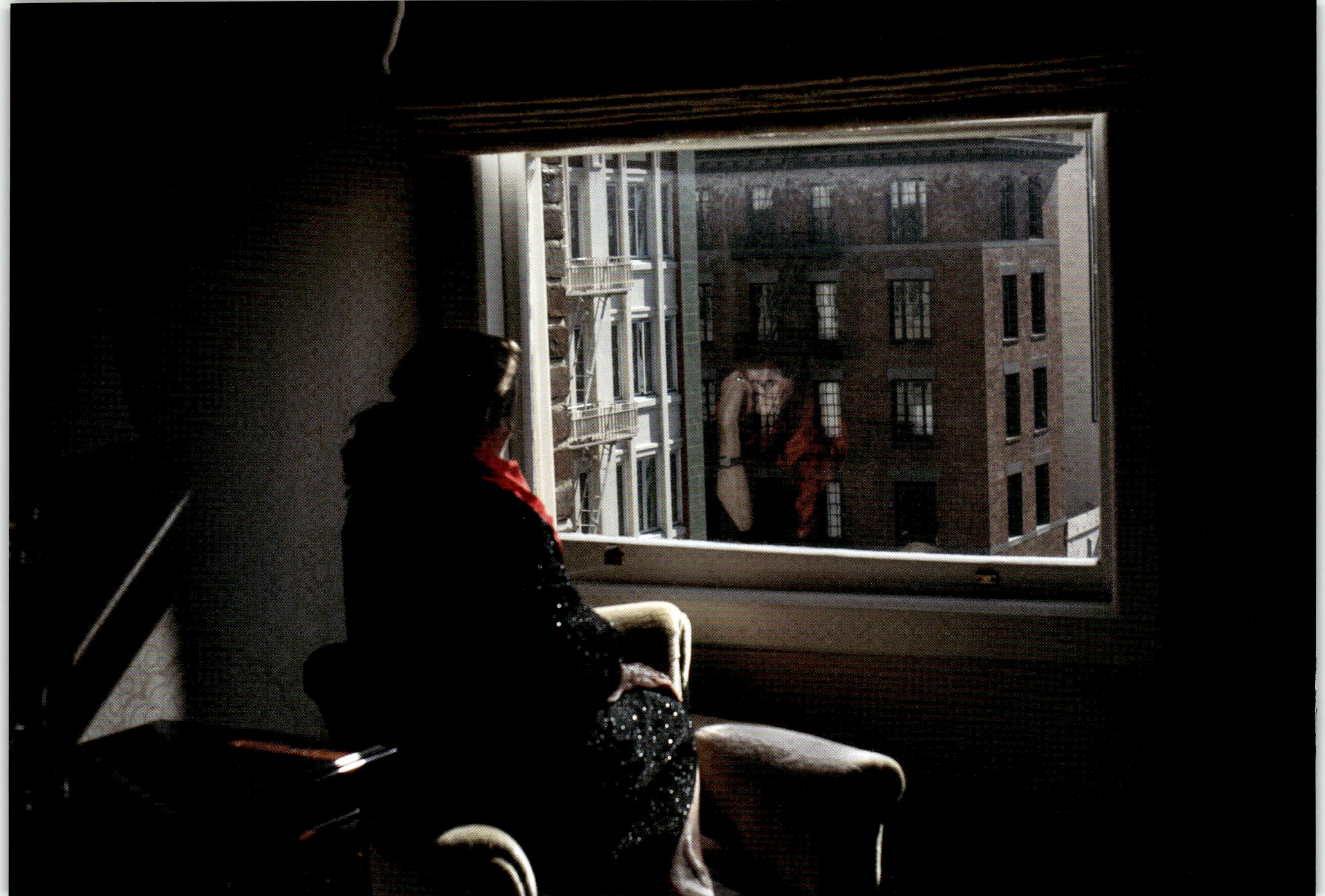

First date. Silent auction. She eyes the red purse—feminine, sexy, eccentric. She's desperate to have it. She bids. She hovers. It's hers!

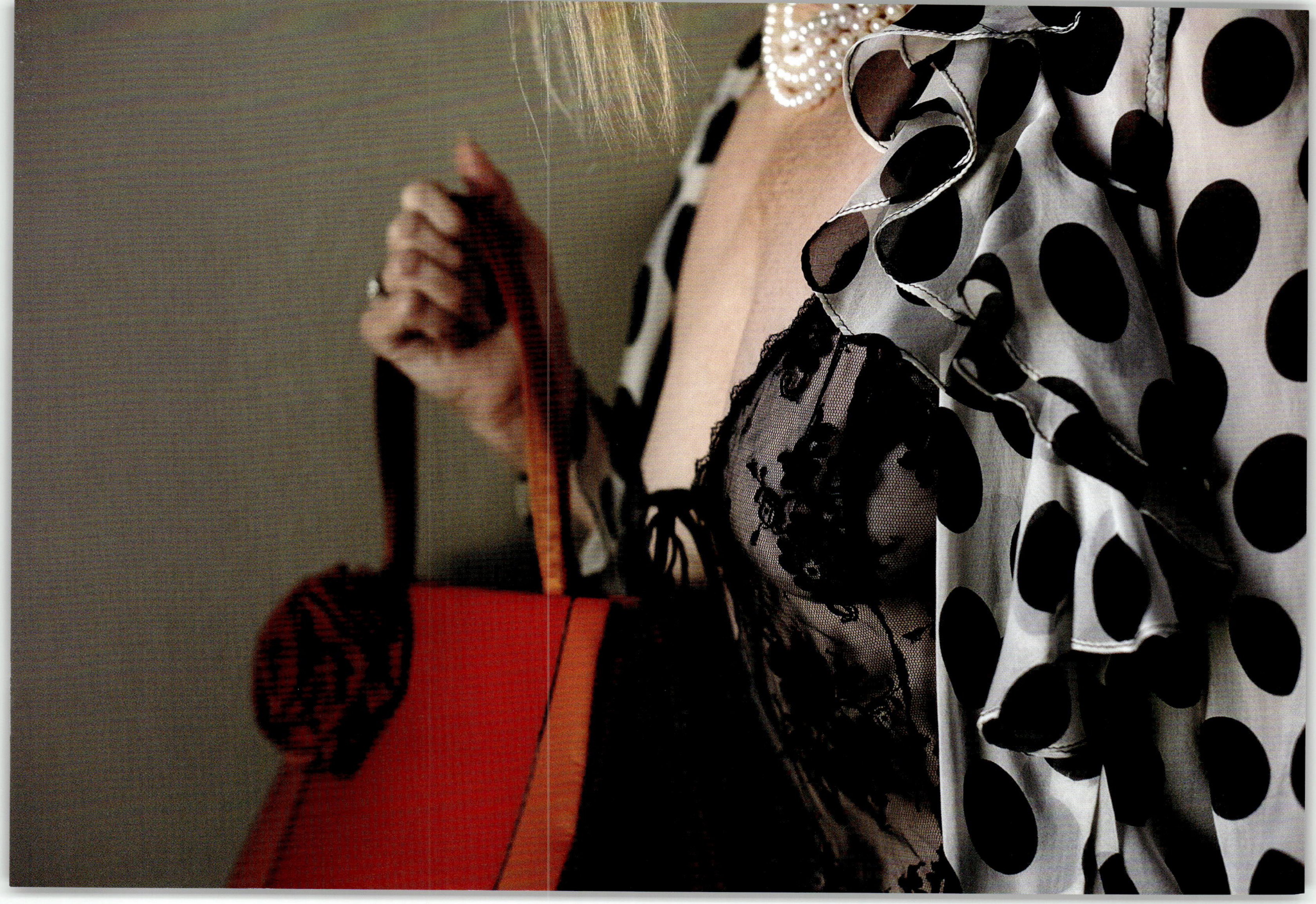

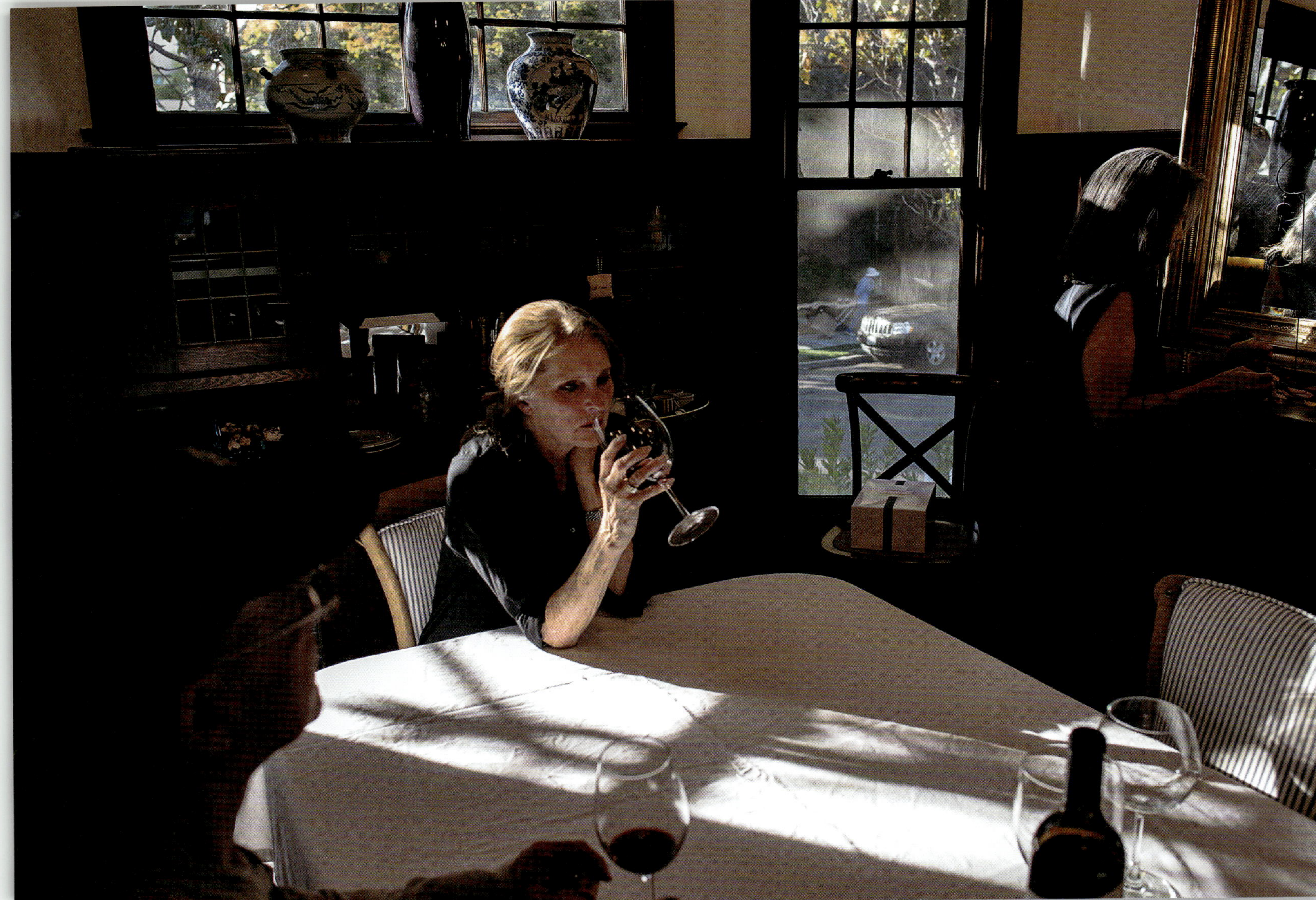

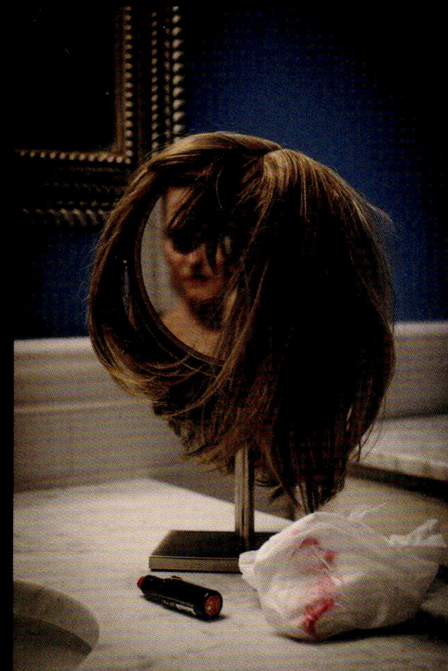

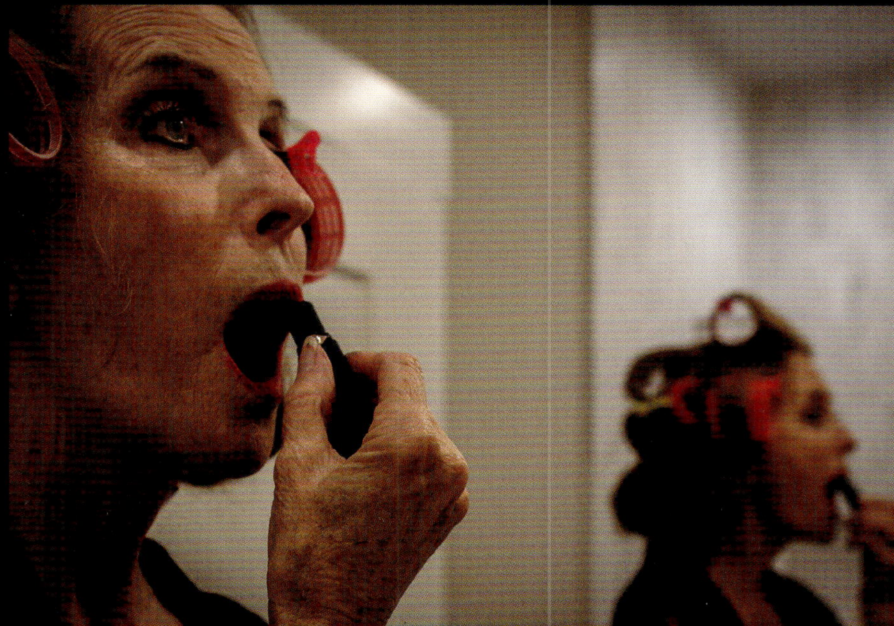

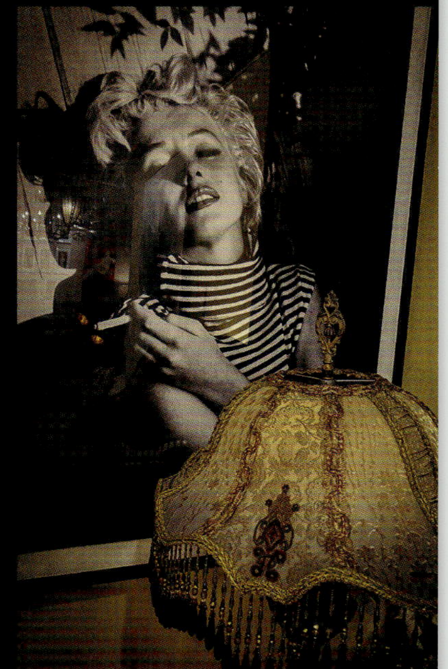

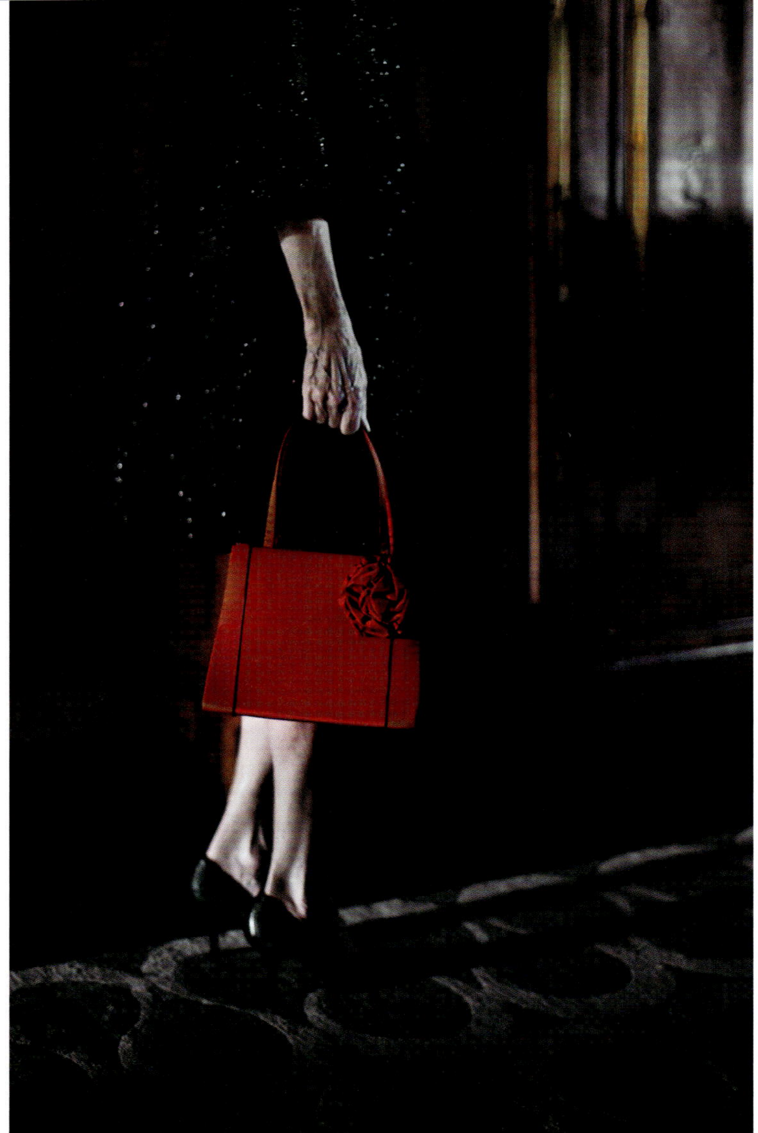

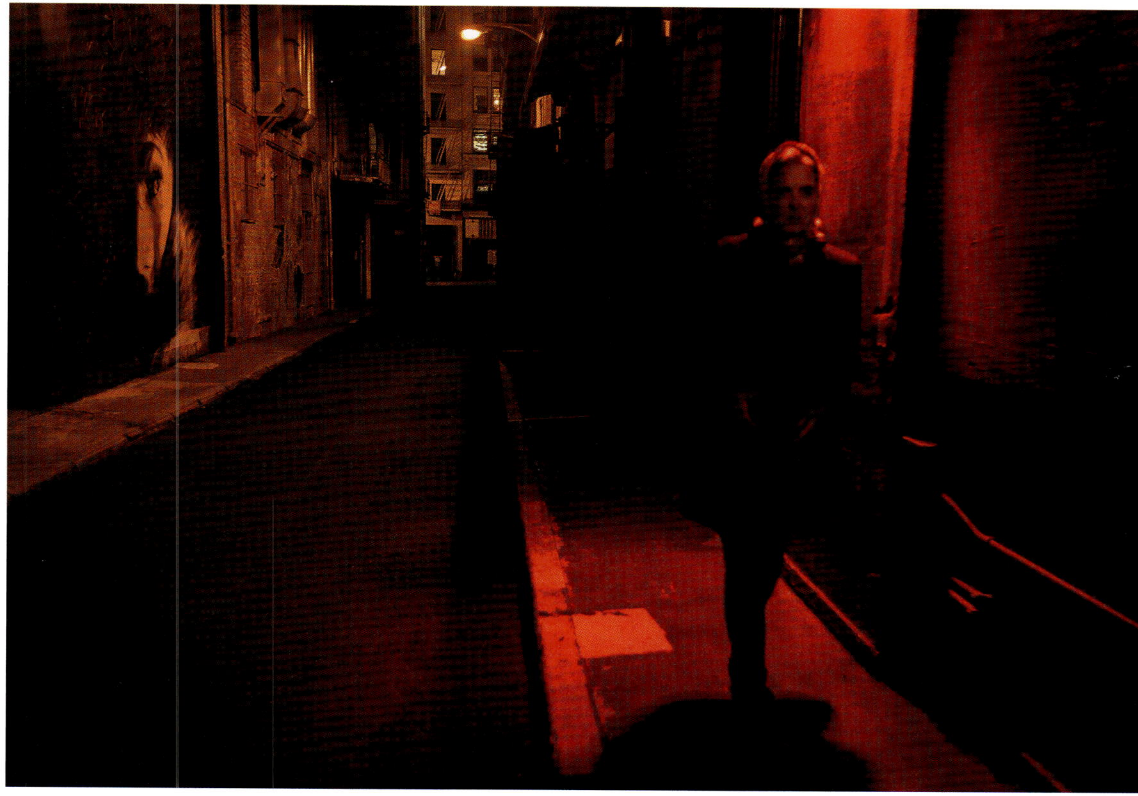

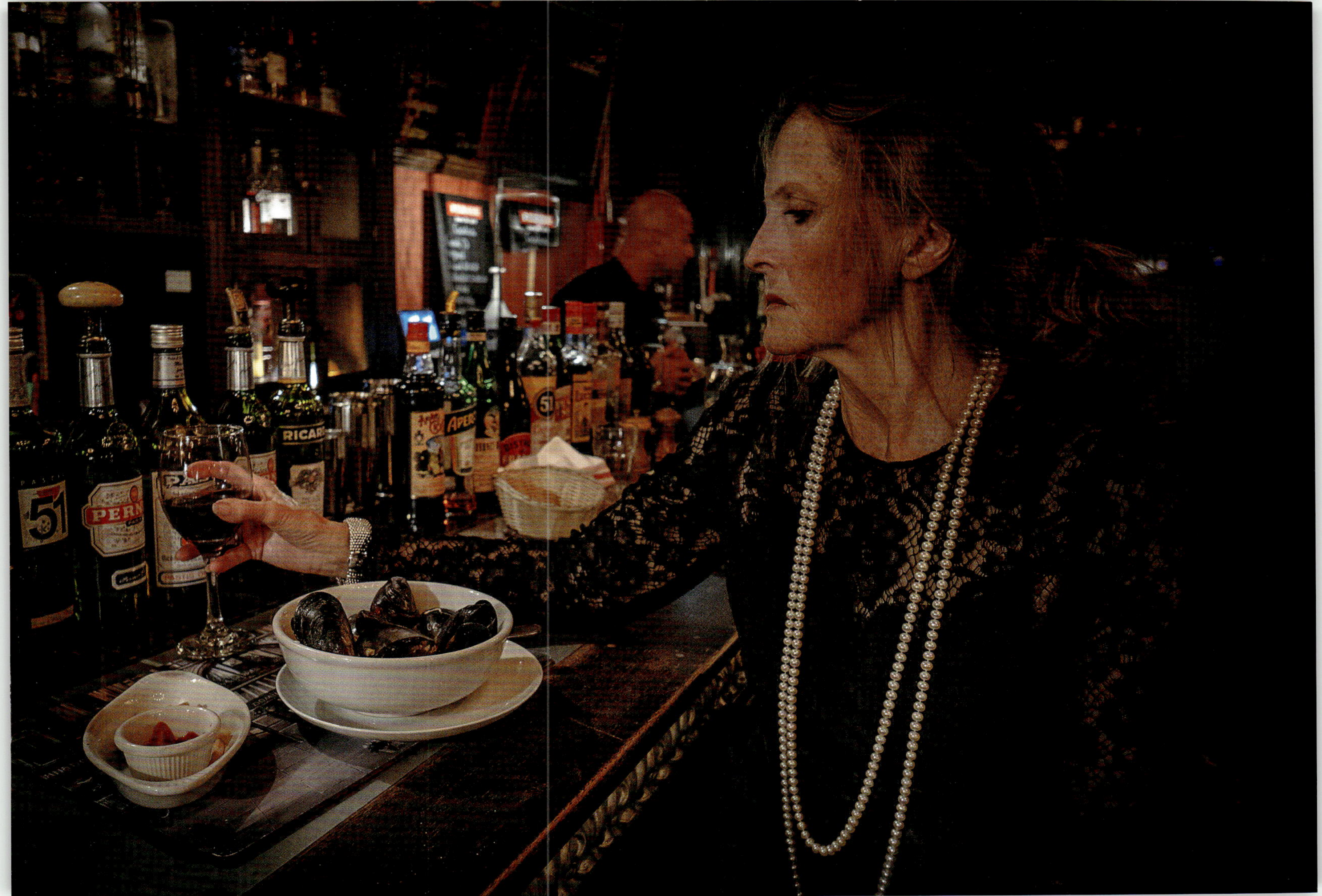
51
RICARD

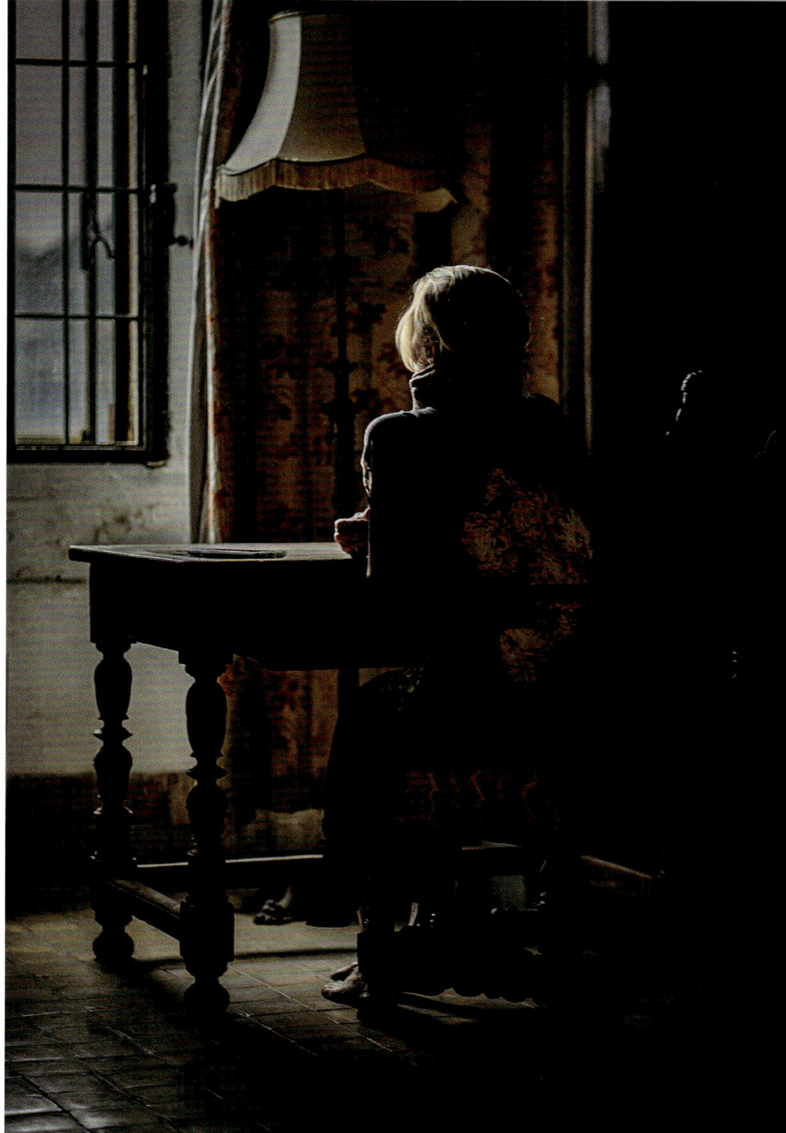

Her grandmother gave her this ballerina doll. One of only a few things left from her childhood. Yet she never displayed her, never cared for her. Why?

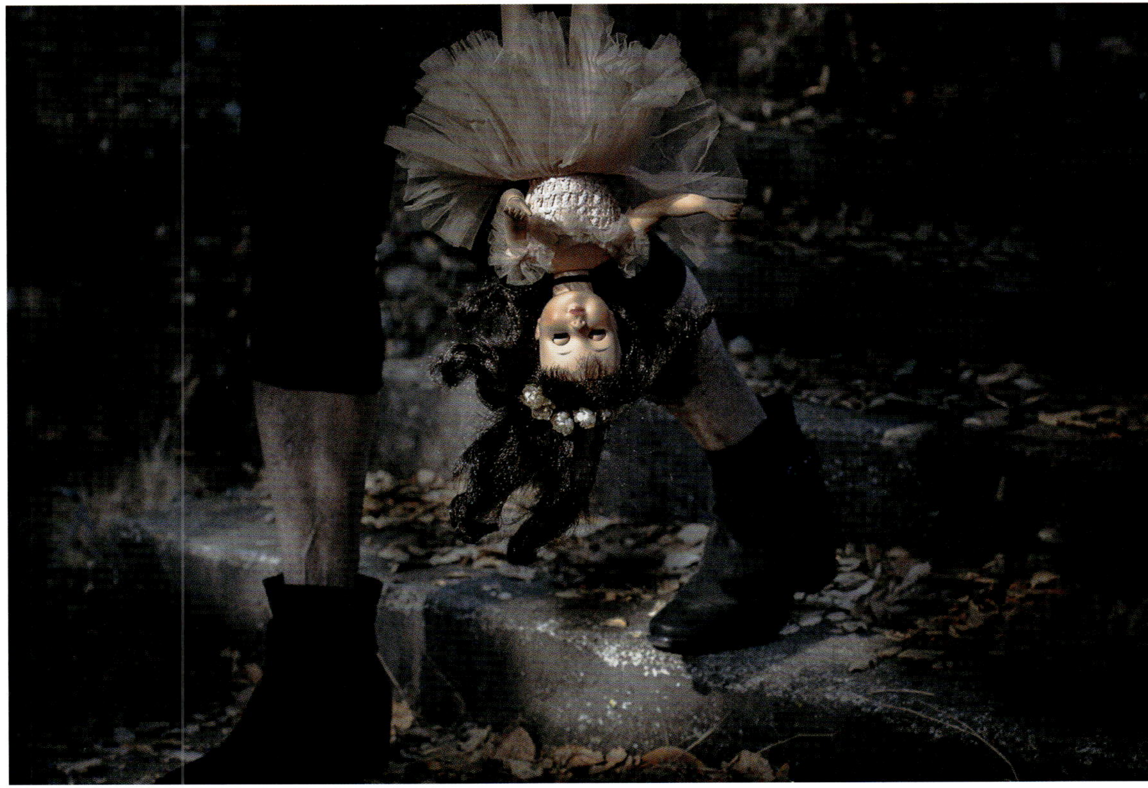

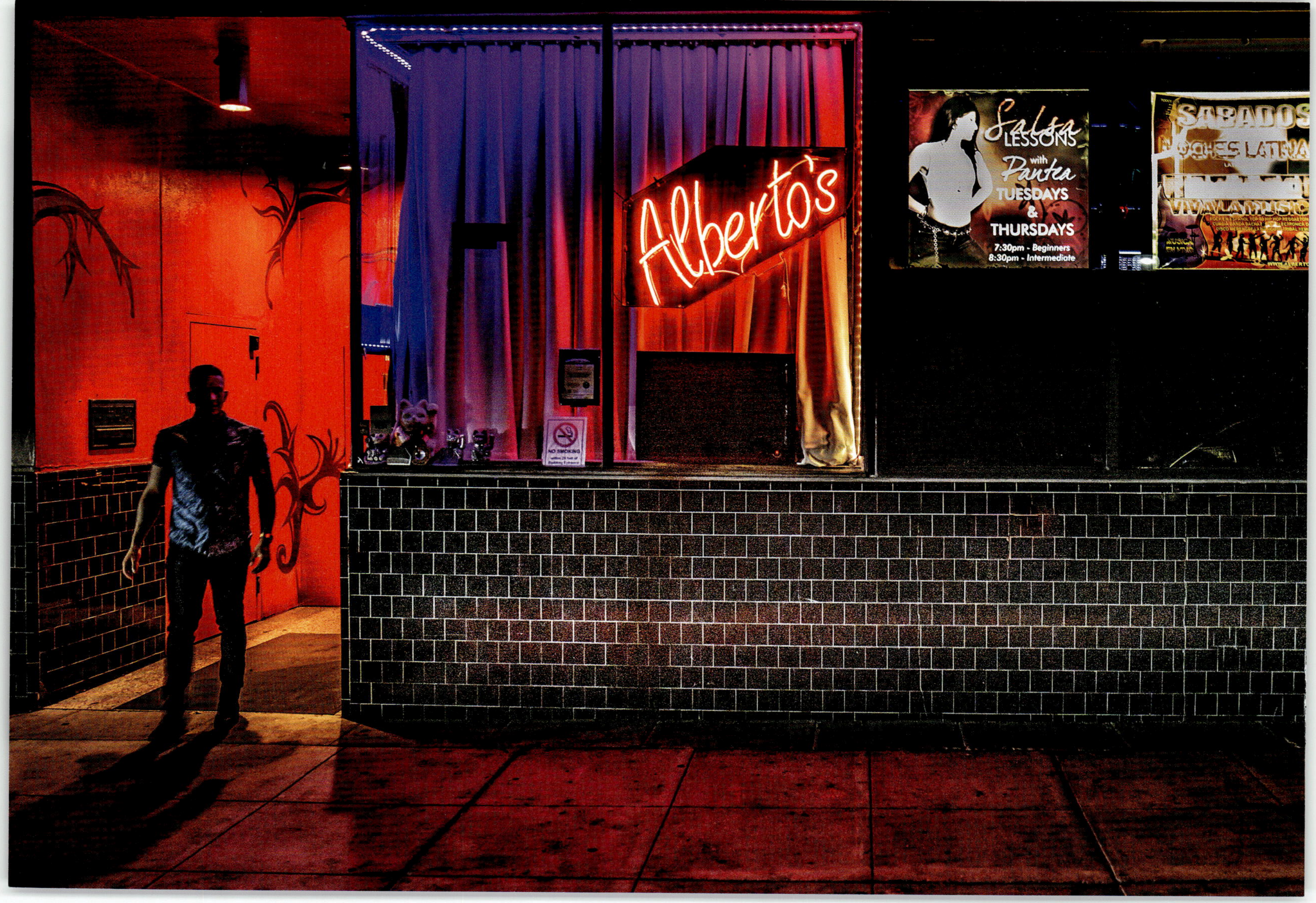
Alberto's
Salsa
LESSONS
with
Pantea
TUESDAYS
&
THURSDAYS
7:30pm - Beginners
8:30pm - Intermediate
SABADOS
NO SMOKING

She leaves at 3:00 a.m. Waiting by the valet stand, quite disheveled, she recognizes the attendant. He smiles at her; he knows. She slinks into the car.

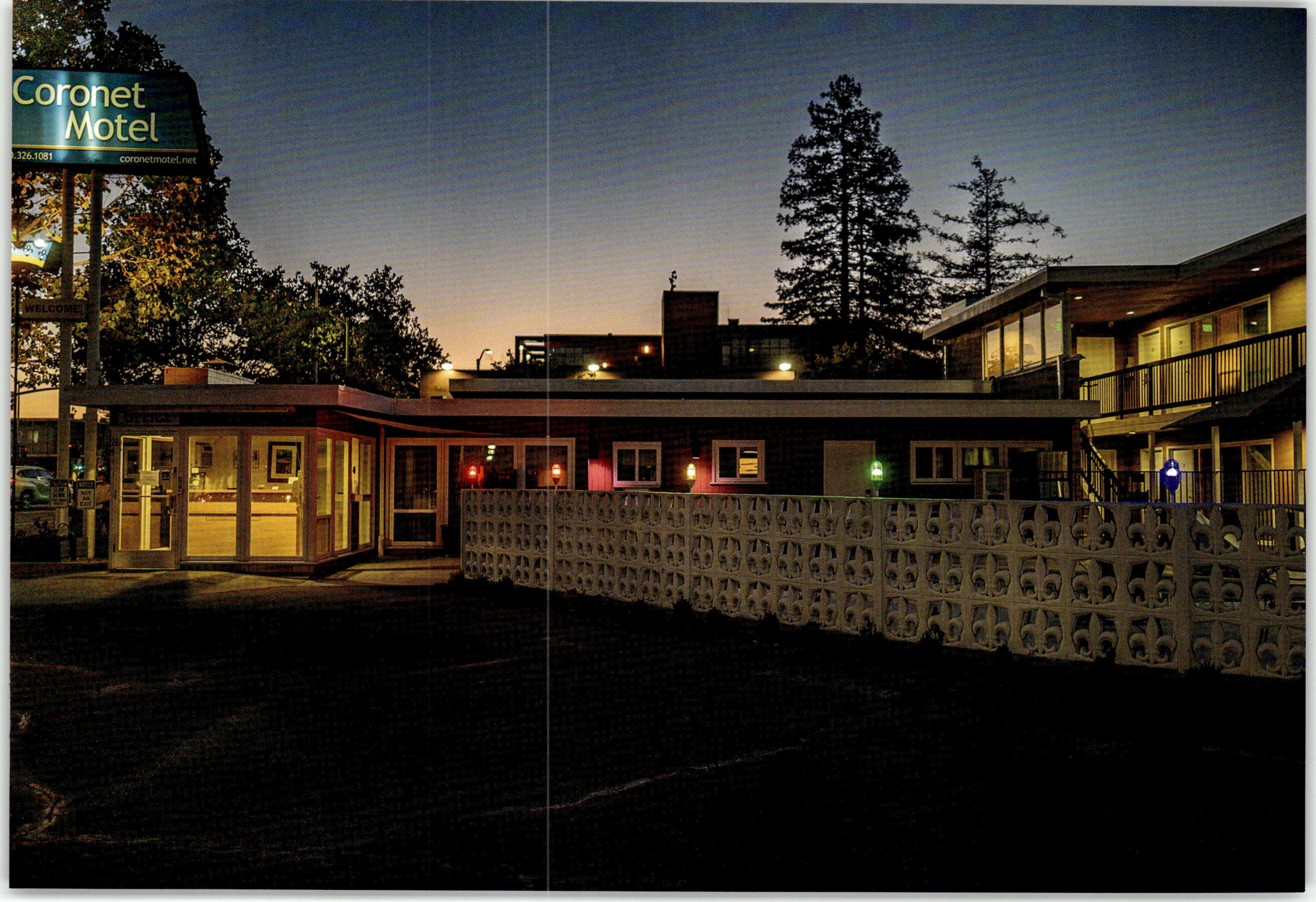
Coronet
Motel
coronetmotel.net
WELCOME

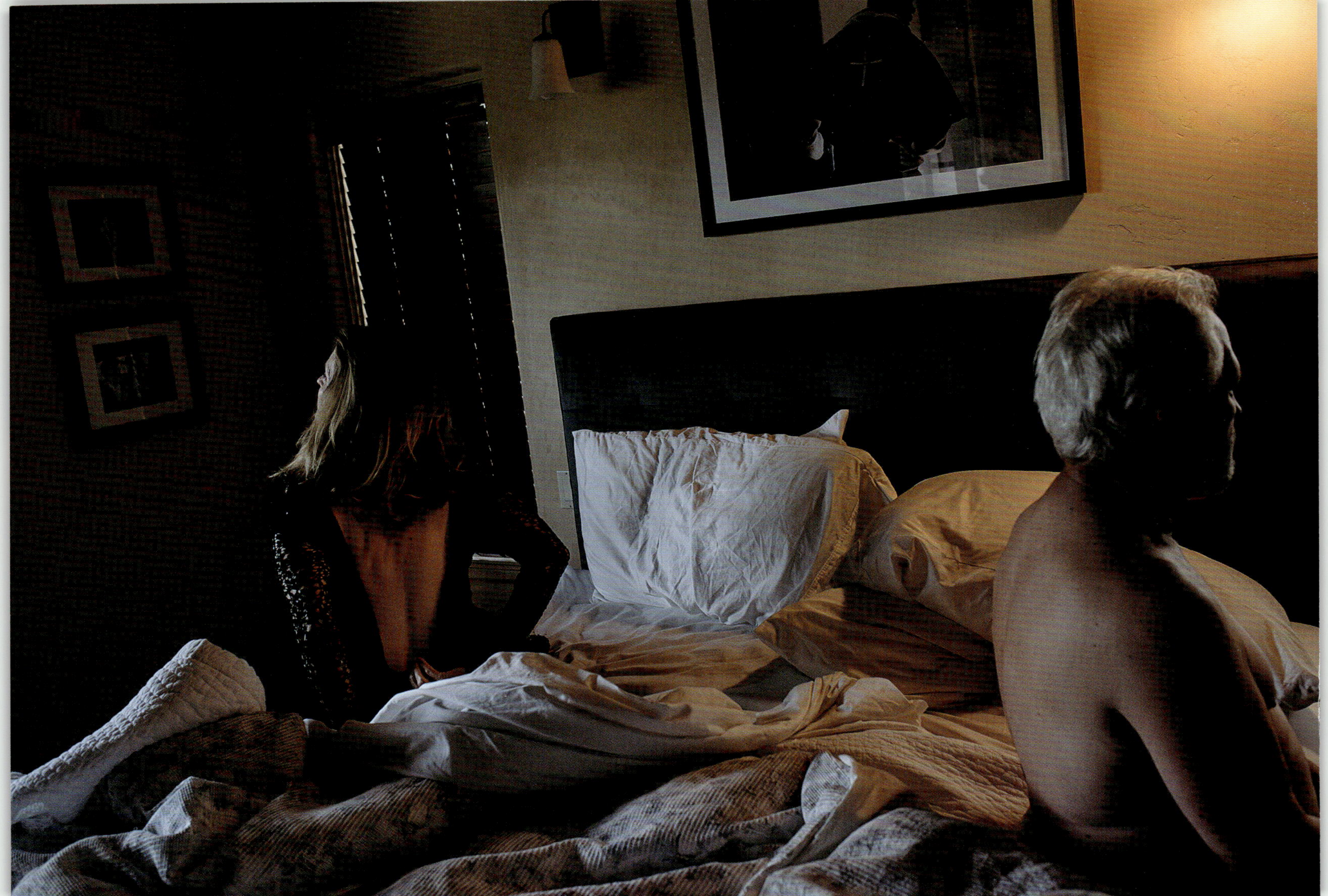

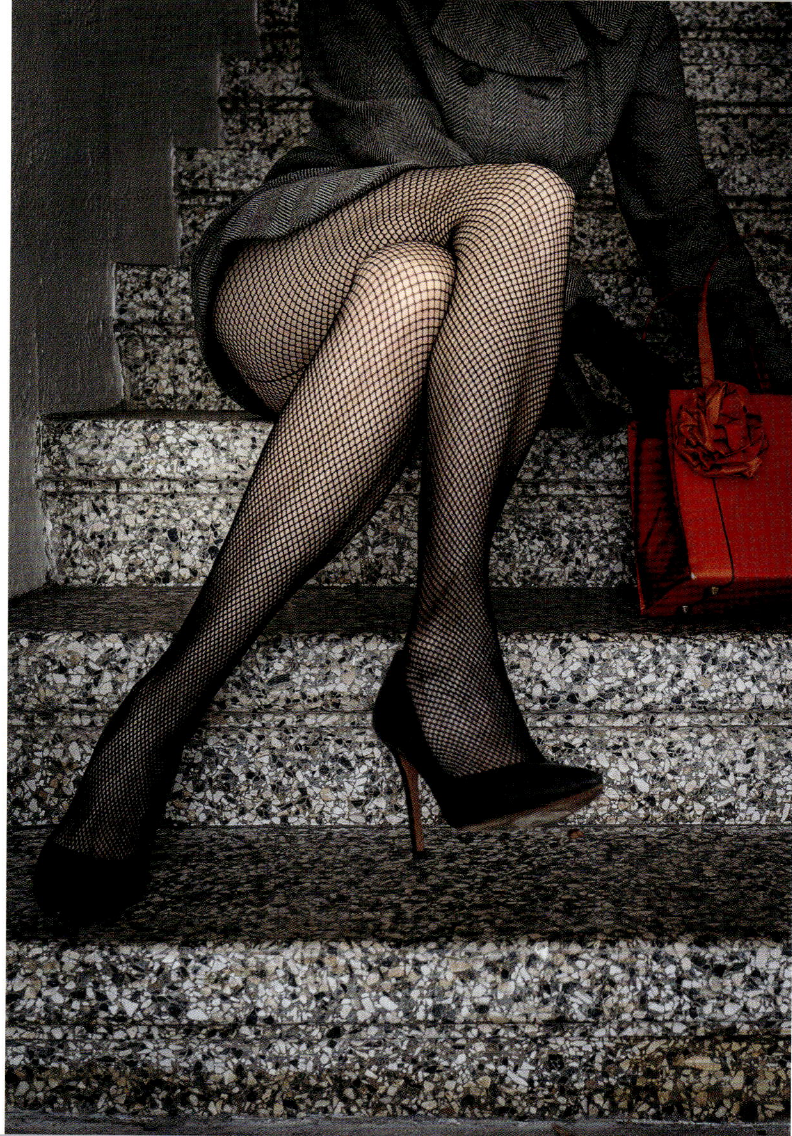

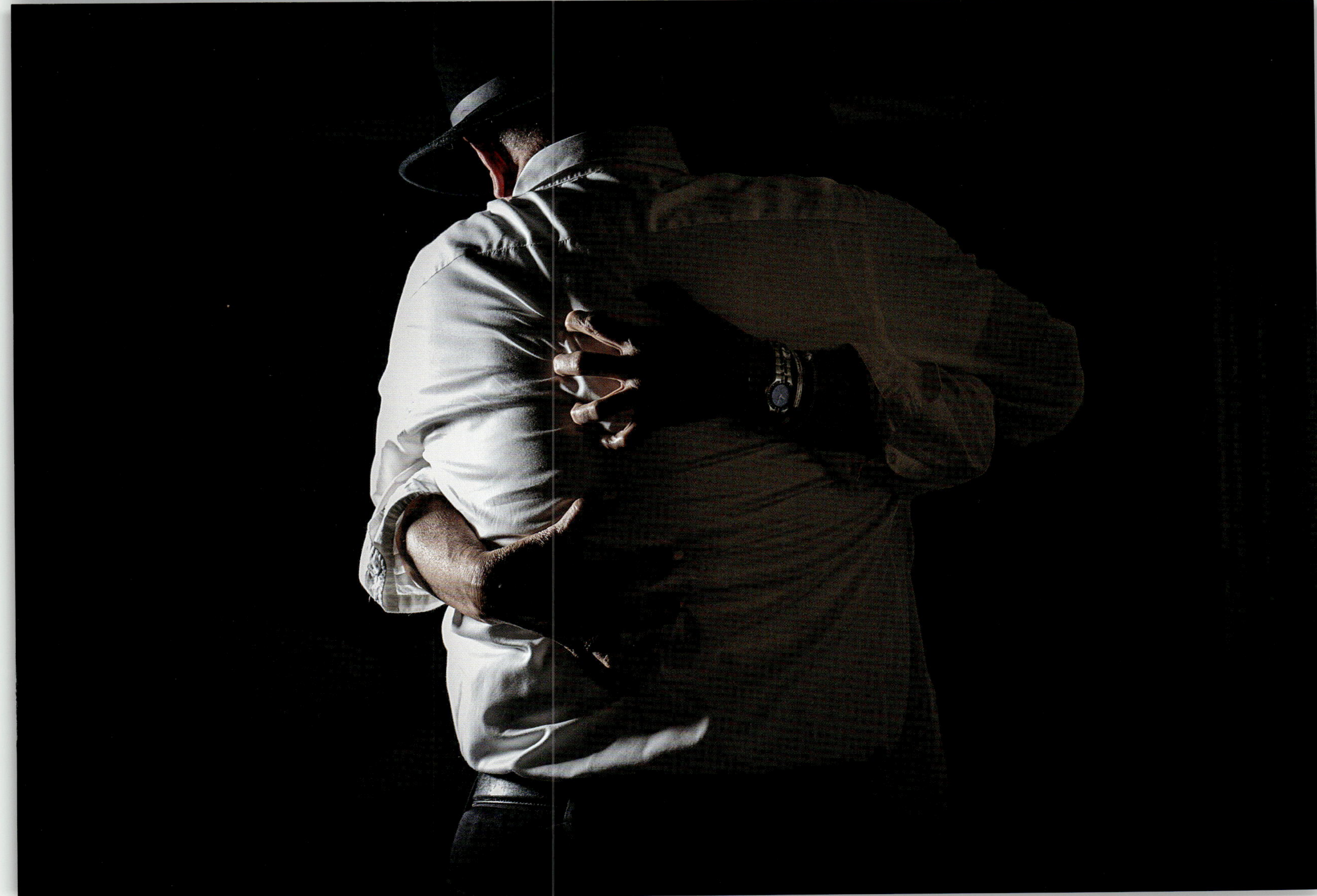

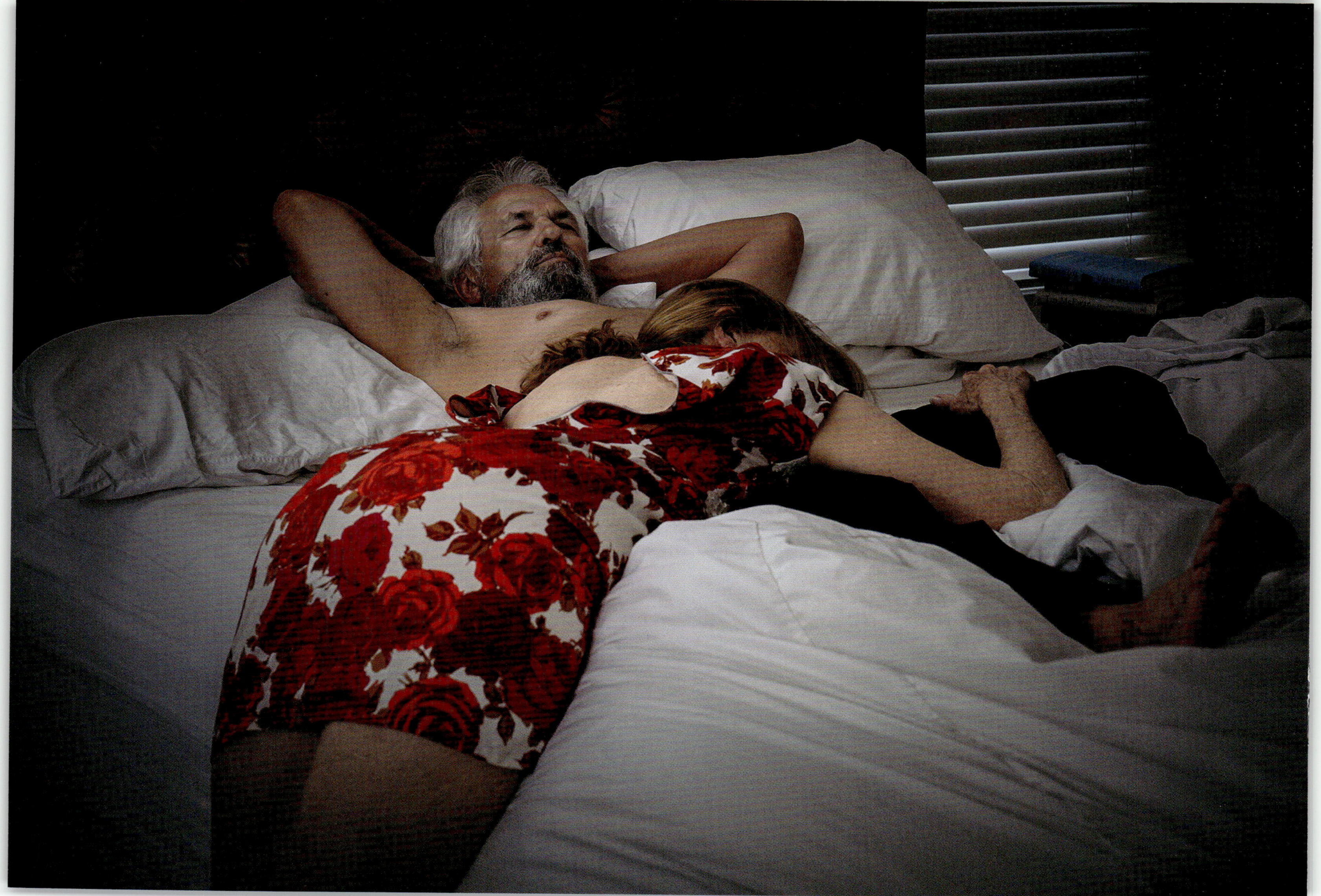

They meet in Room 24. She dims the lights, lights the candles, afraid to show her lived-in body. He says, rather abruptly, "I can't see a thing in here. Where are the lights?"

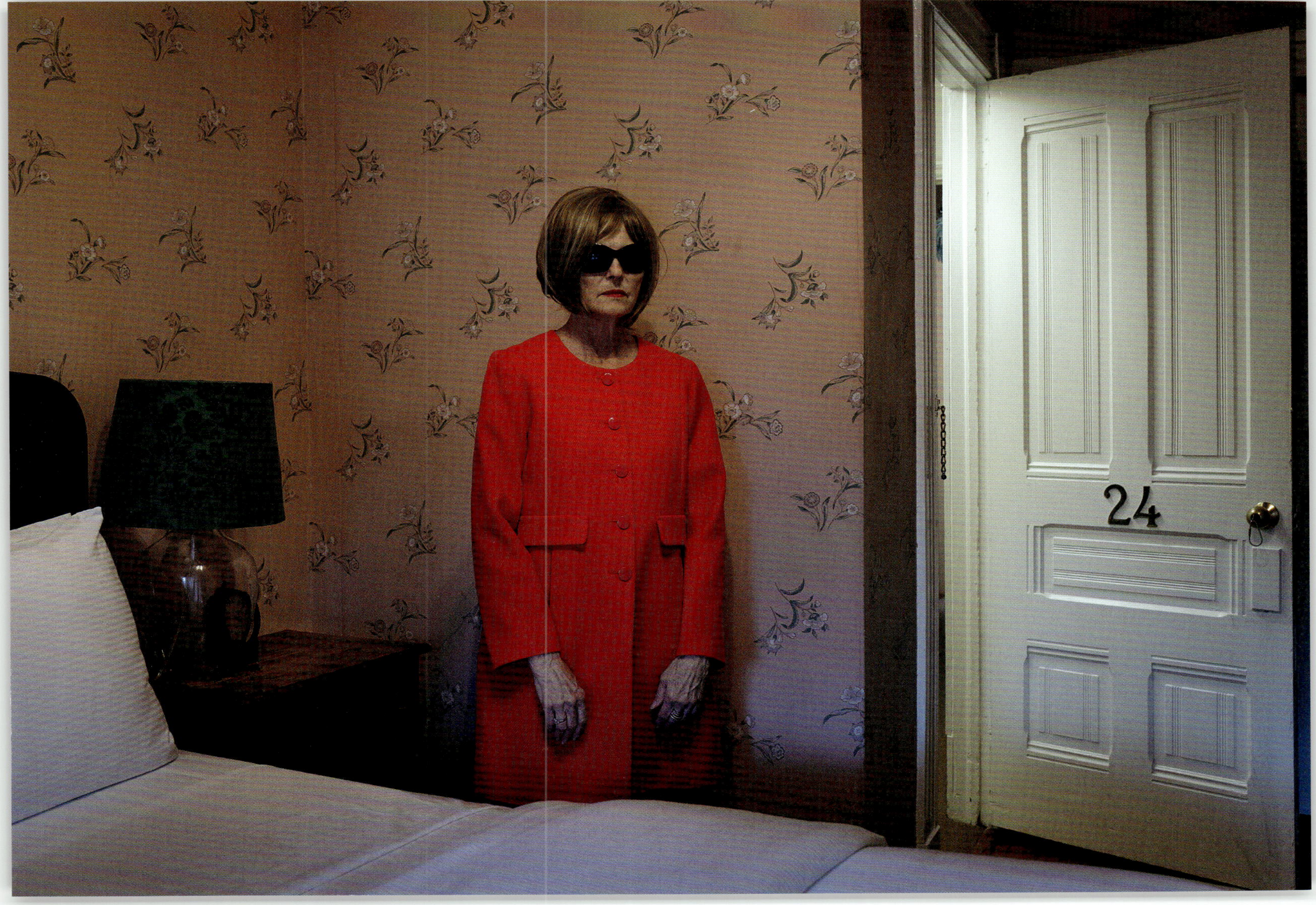
24

*"She wore blue velvet /
bluer than velvet was
the night," she sings,
using her hairbrush as
a microphone, watching
herself in the mirror. Raw
and emotional, it takes
her mind to another place.
She needs this escape.*

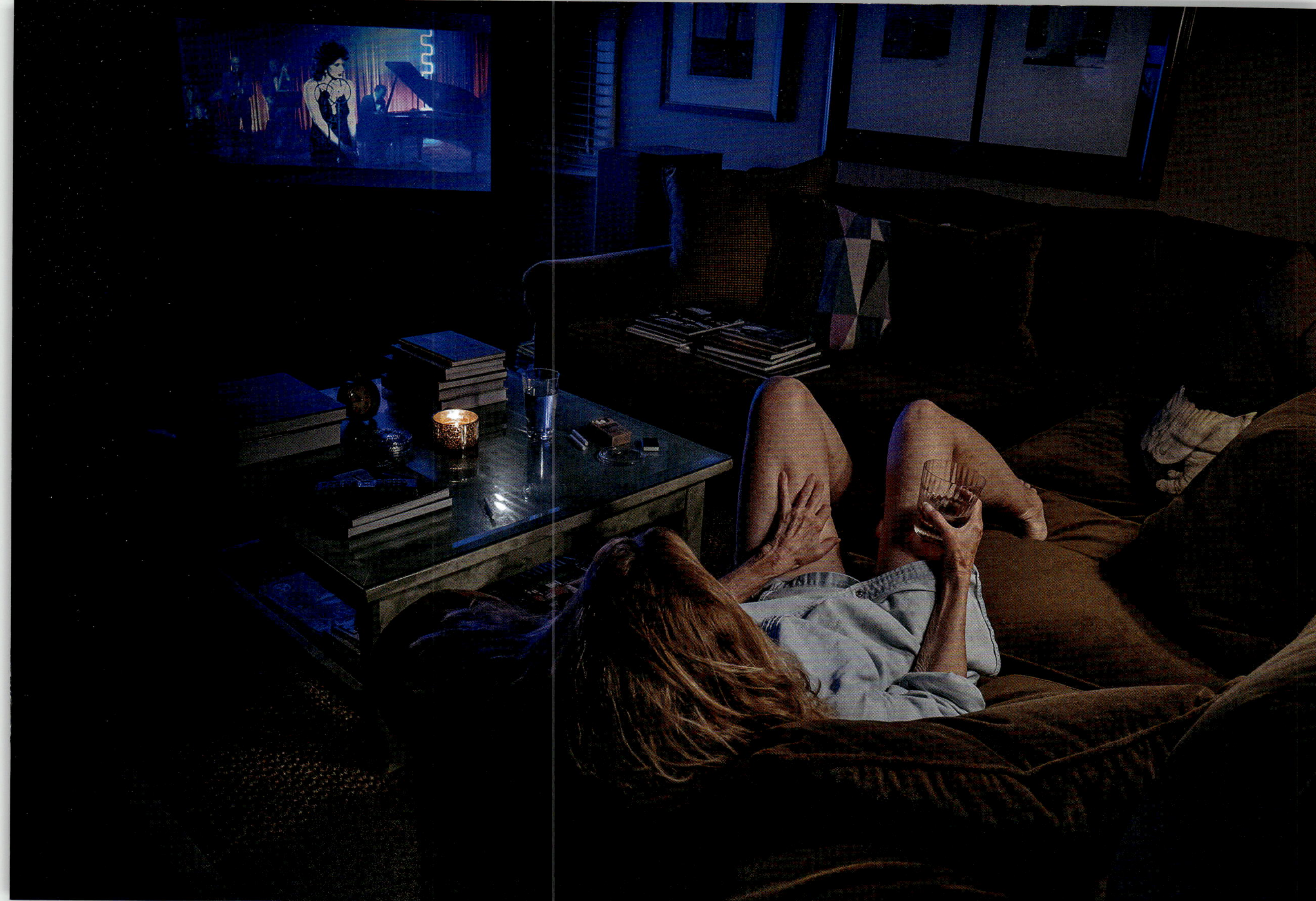

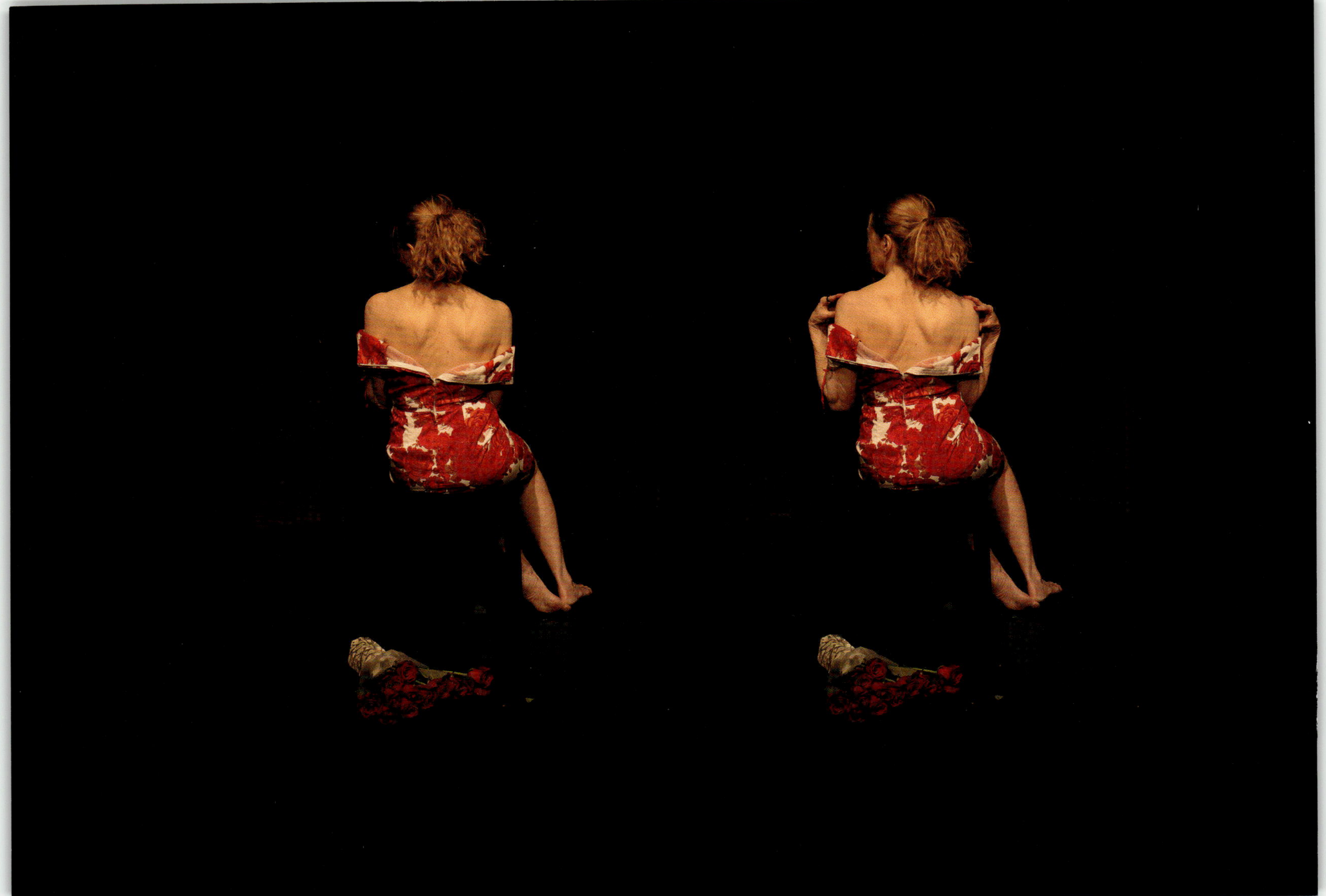

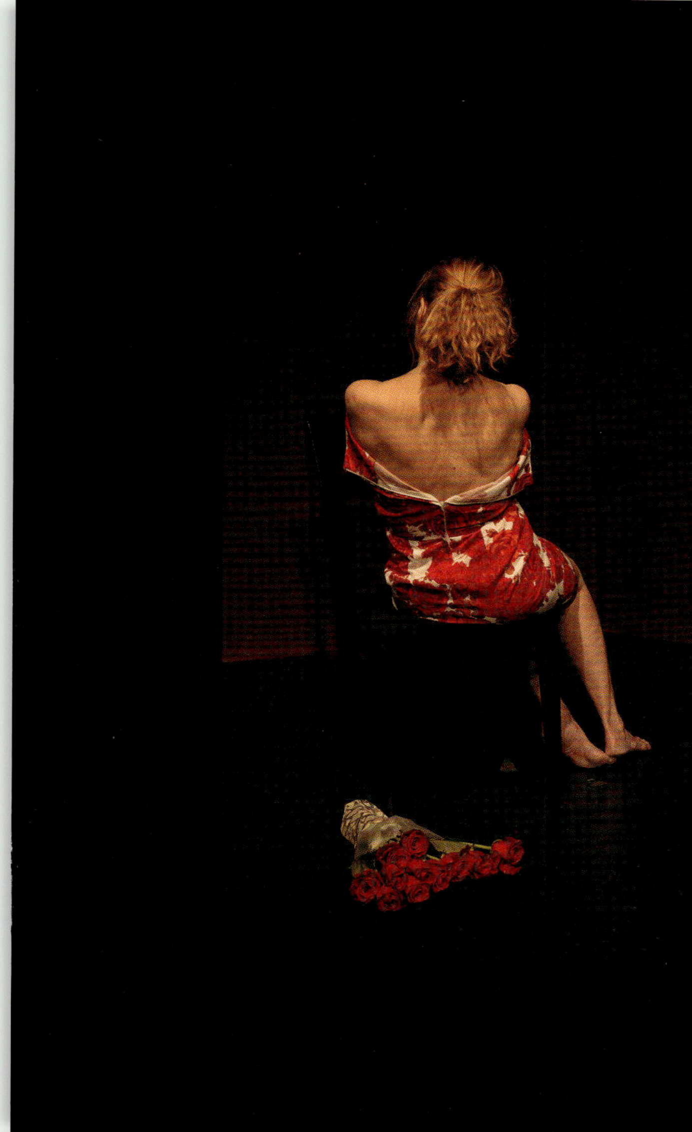

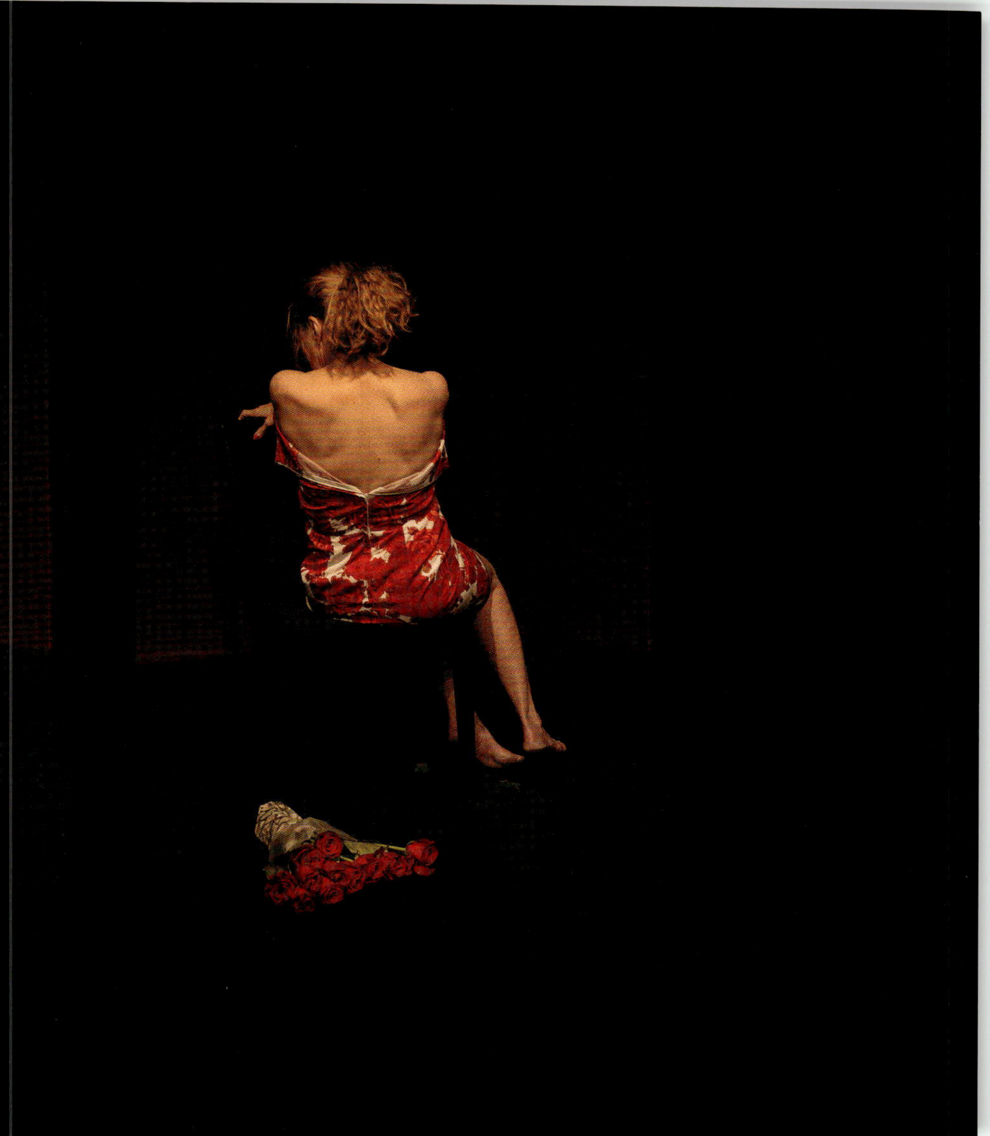

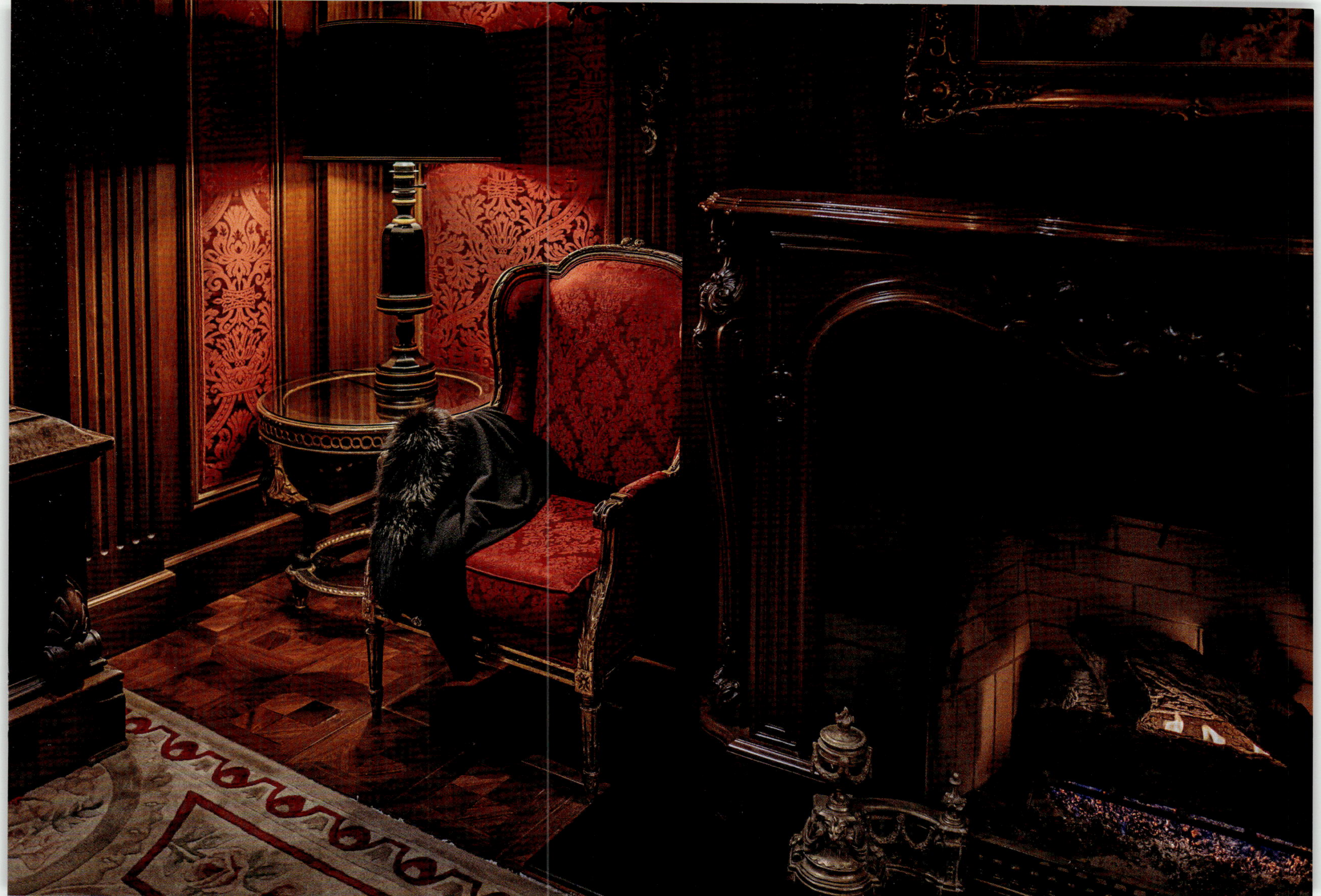

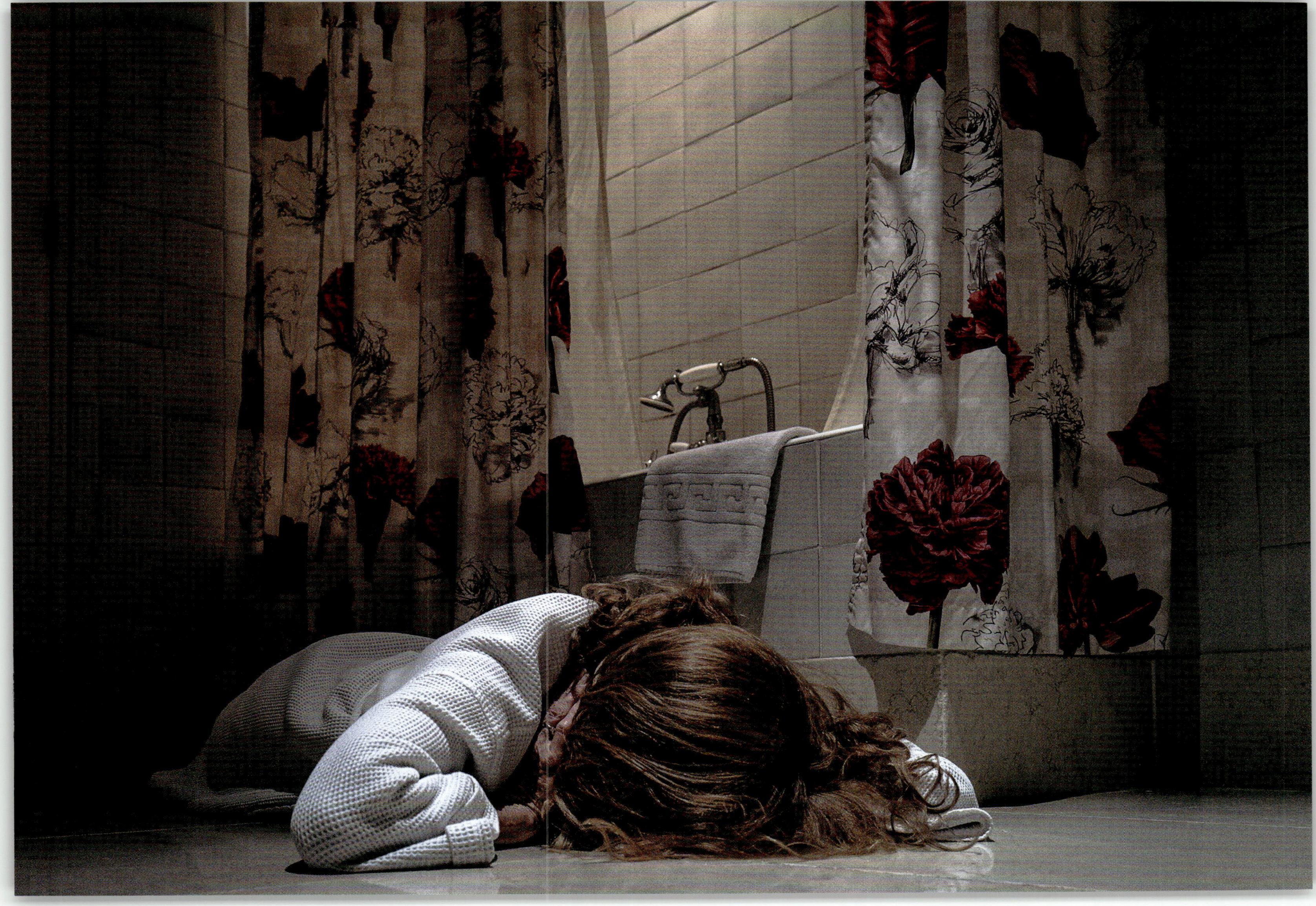

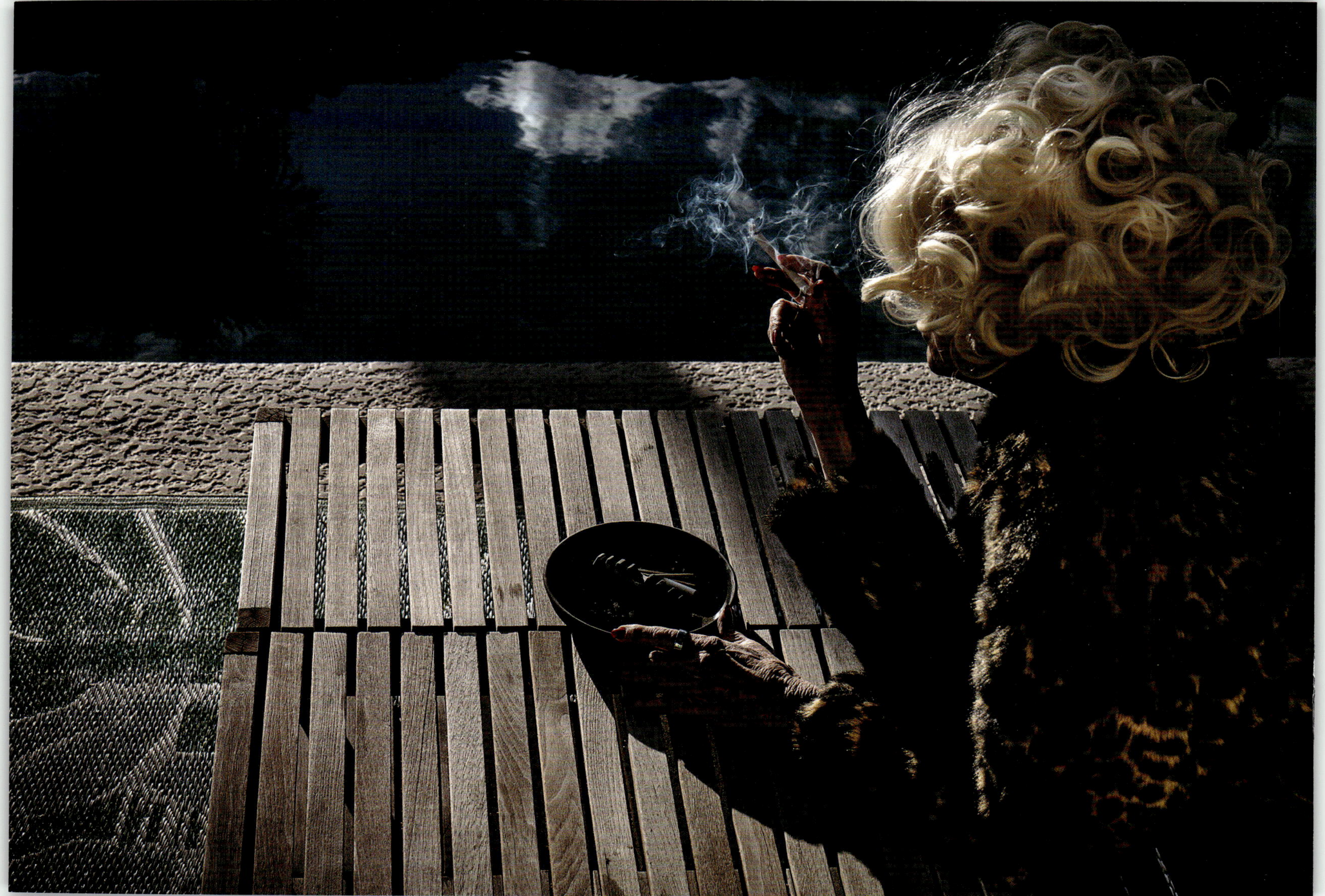

She finds herself obsessed with Marilyn Monroe— her sexuality, femme-fatale mystique, and tragic life. Comforting to know she wasn't alone with such an untimely death. She visits Helena Drive to see where it ended.

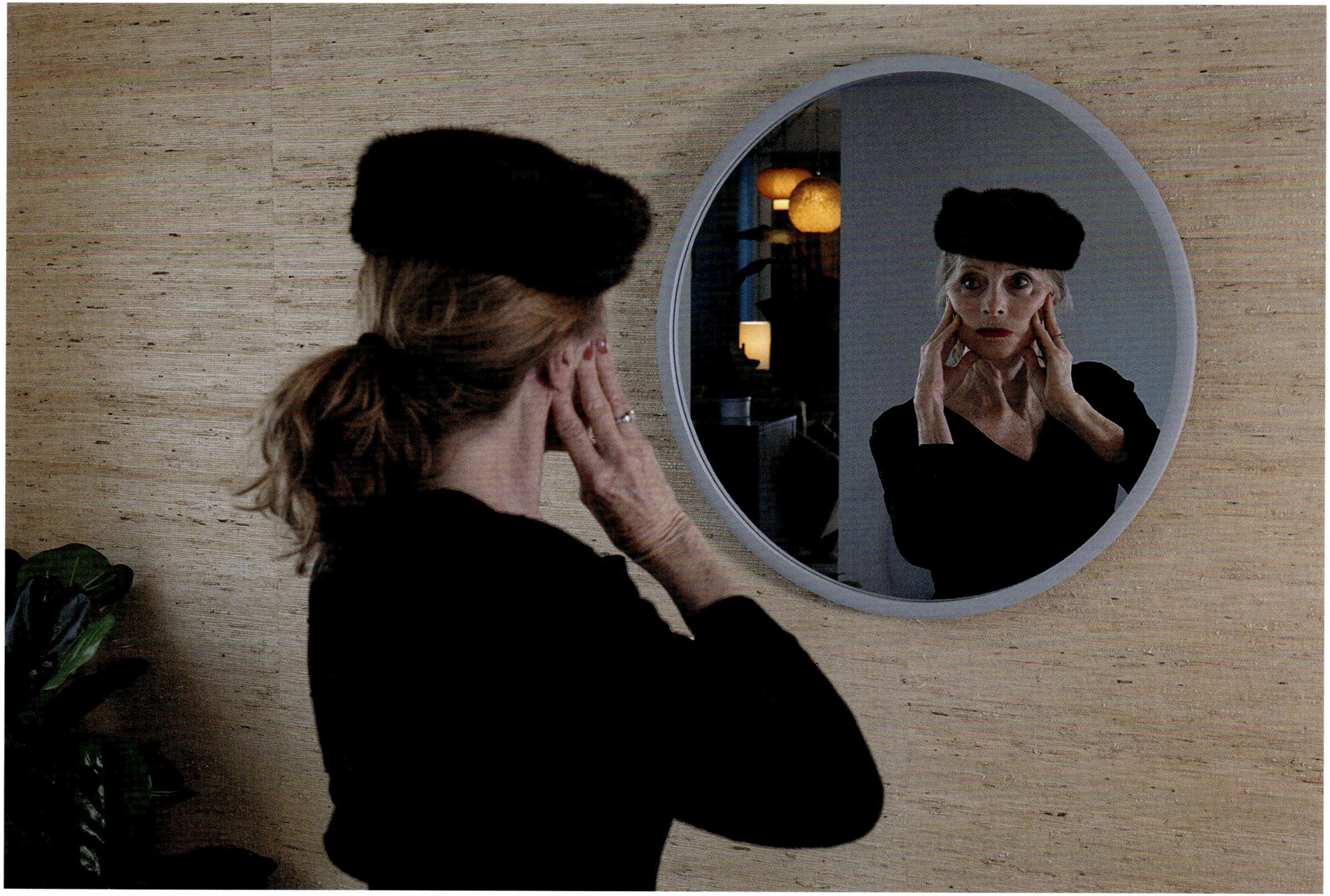

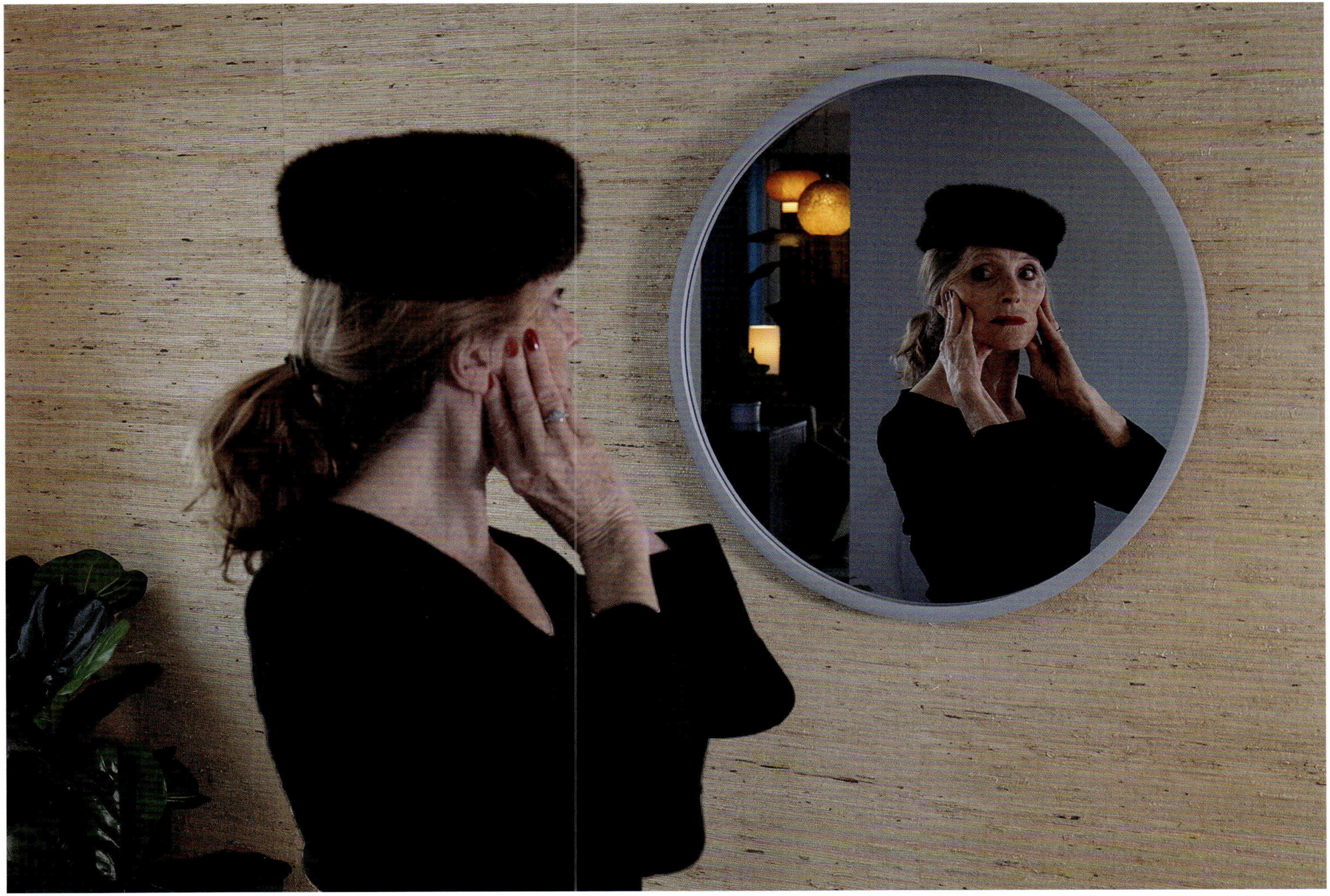

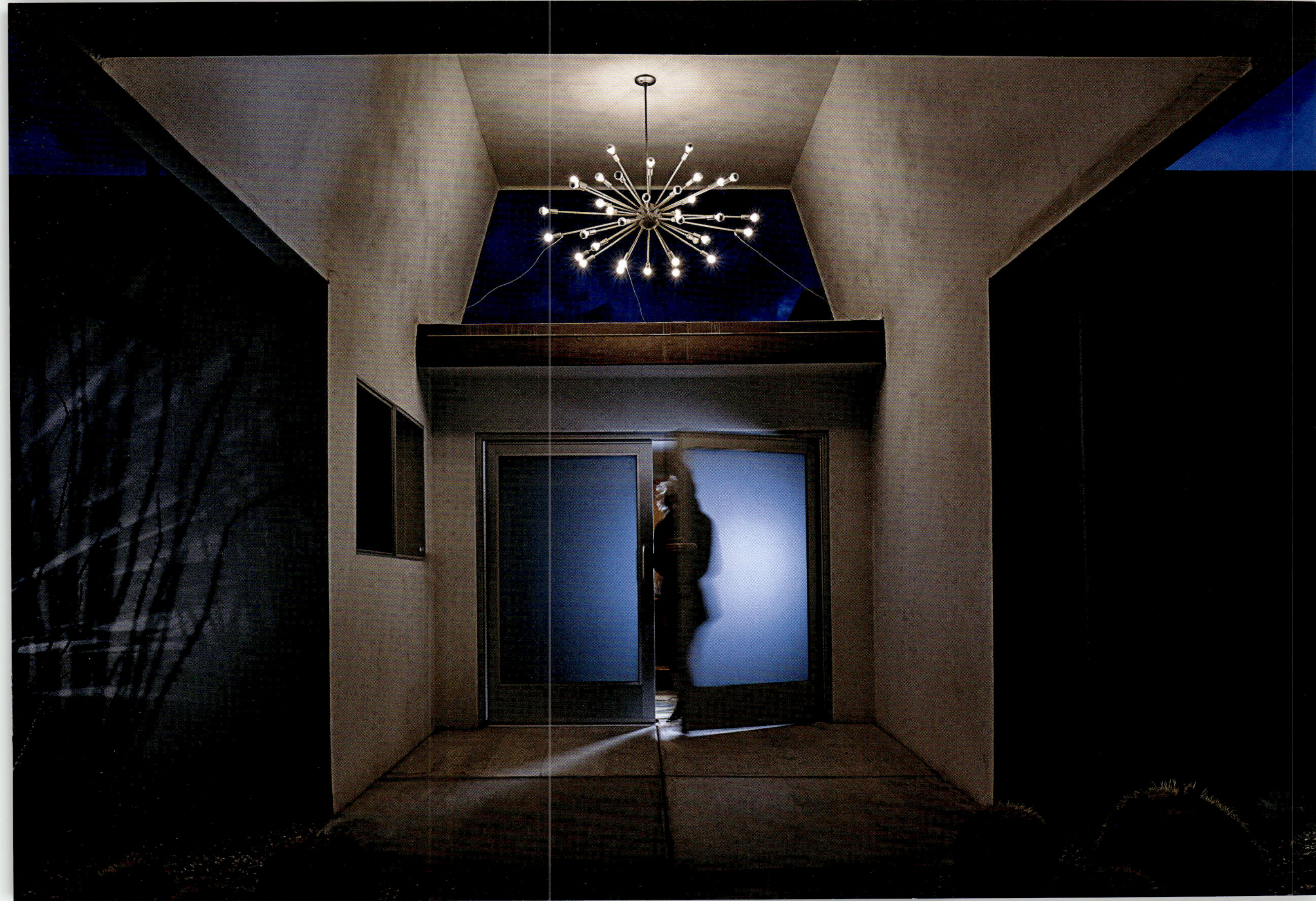

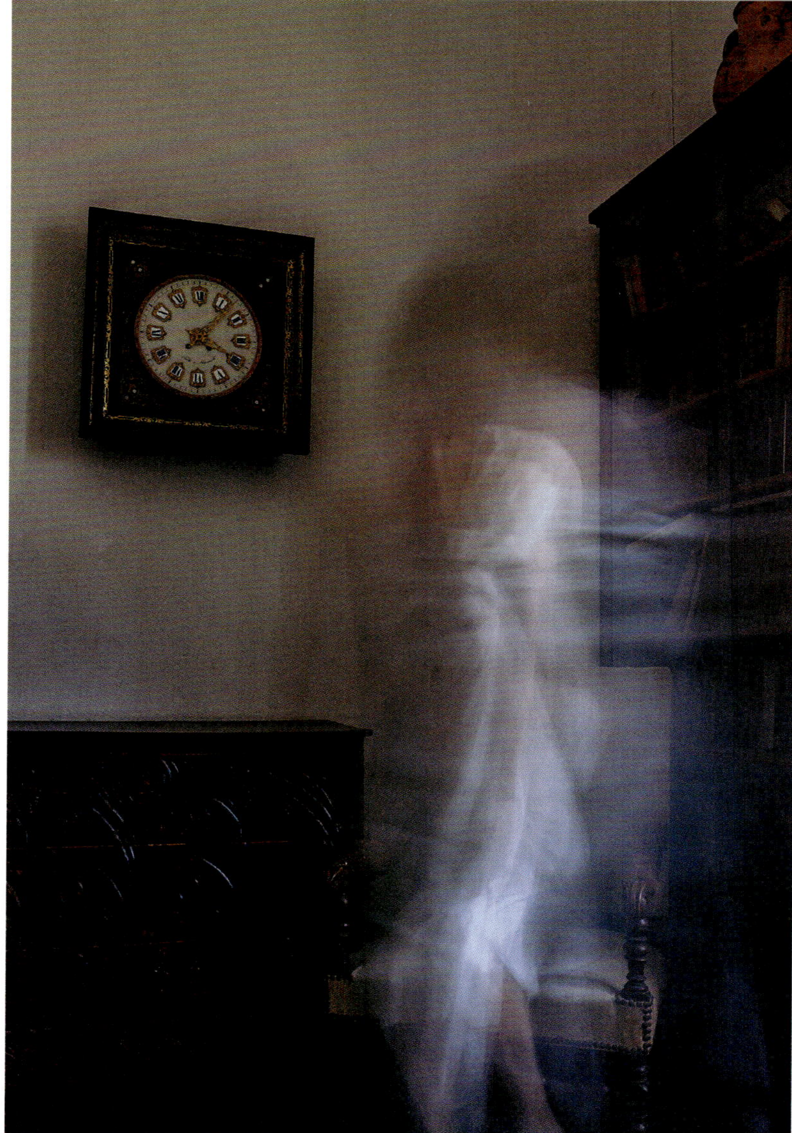

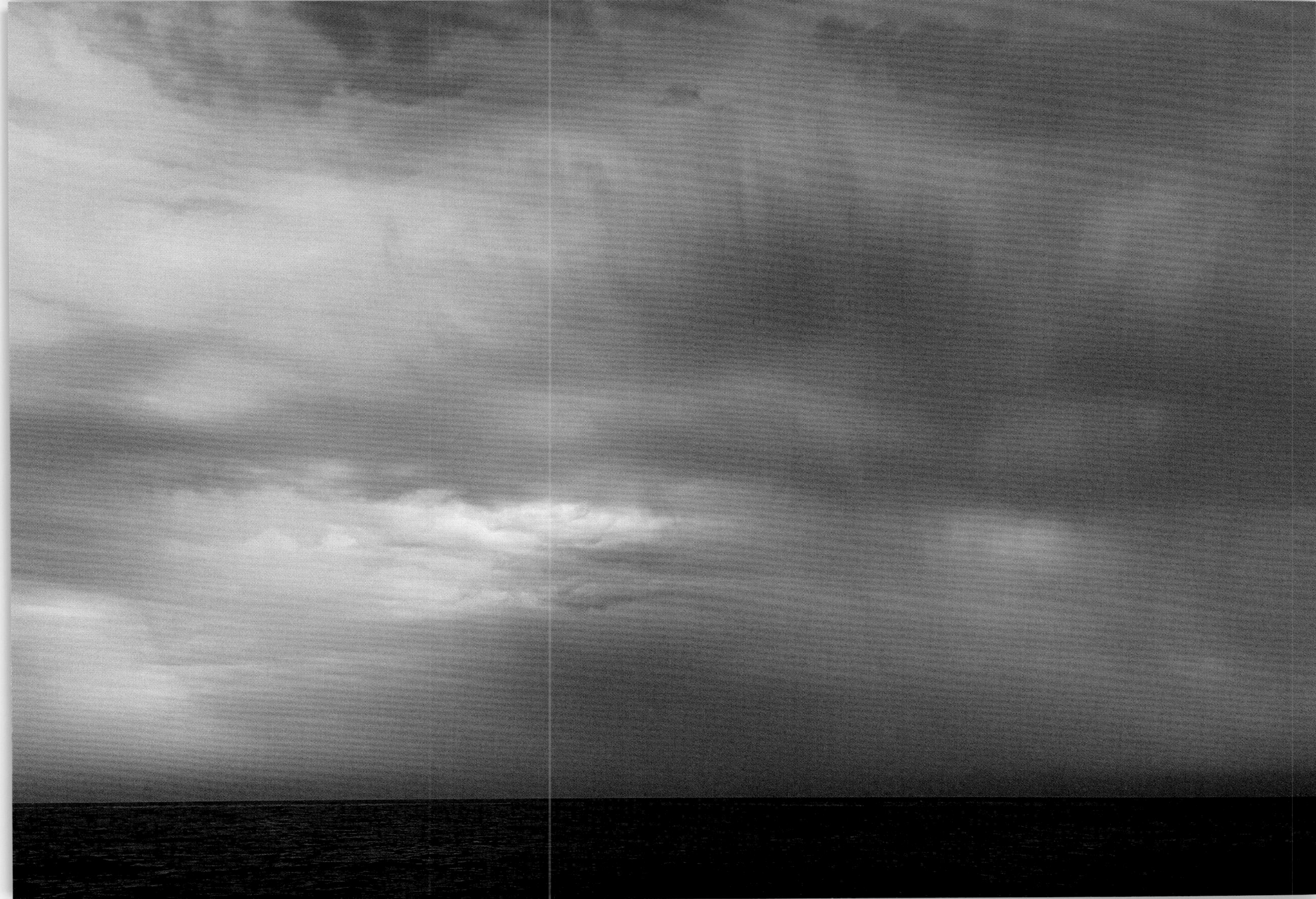

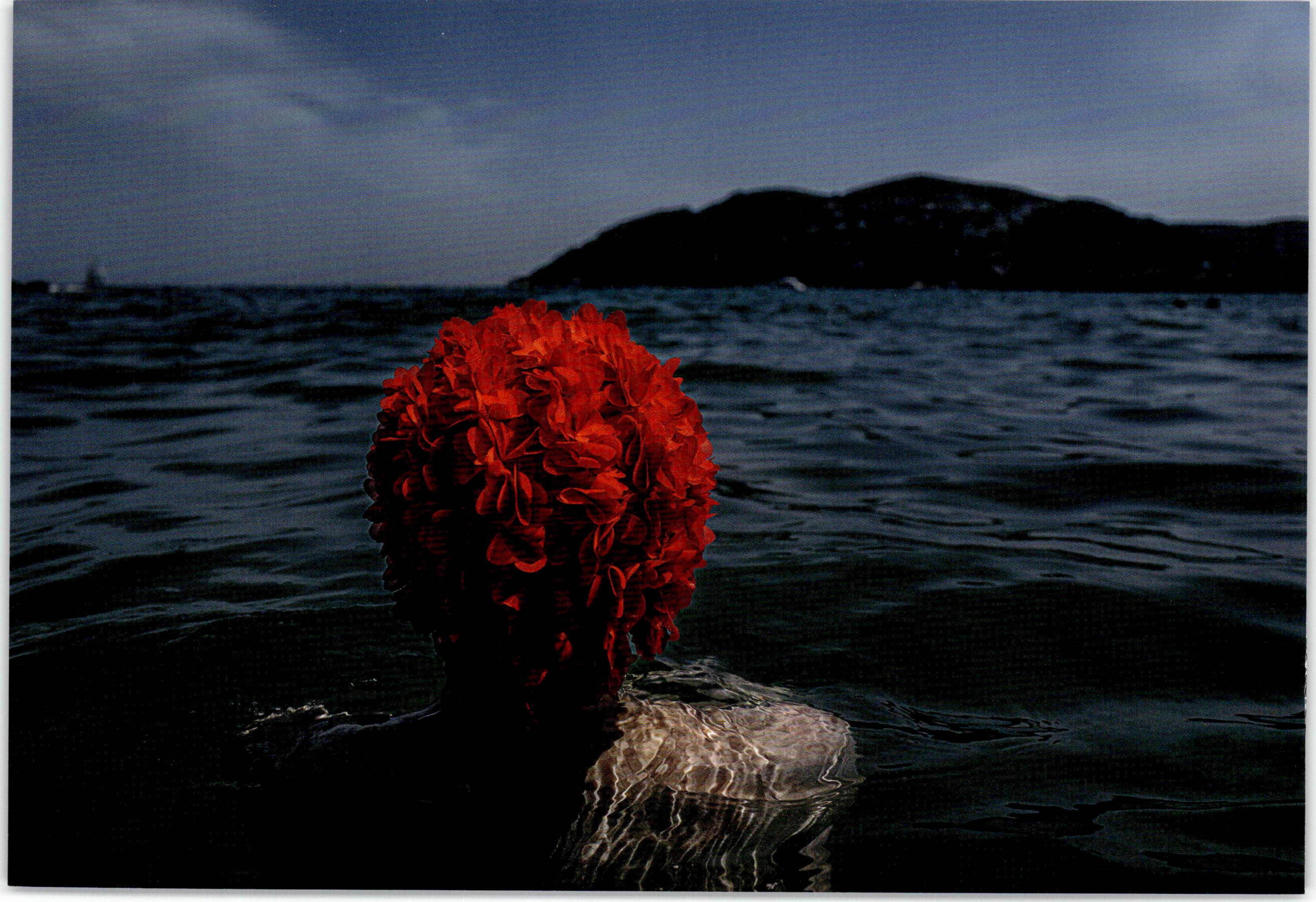

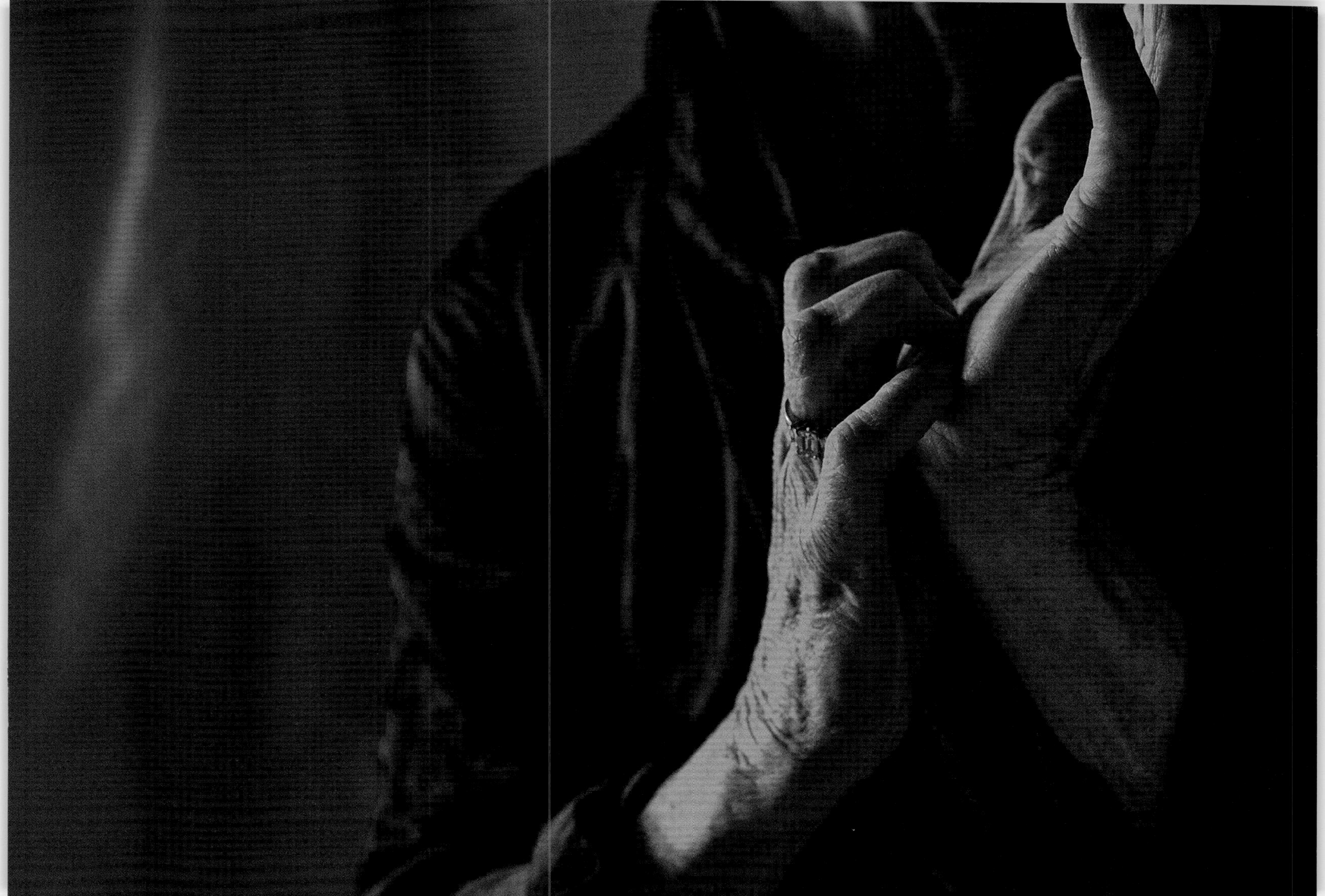

And the Match.com
date with the doctor
whose young French wife
has just dumped him.
The date is going fine
until he turns to her,
clearly disappointed:
"You look so much older
than your picture." She
is five years his junior.

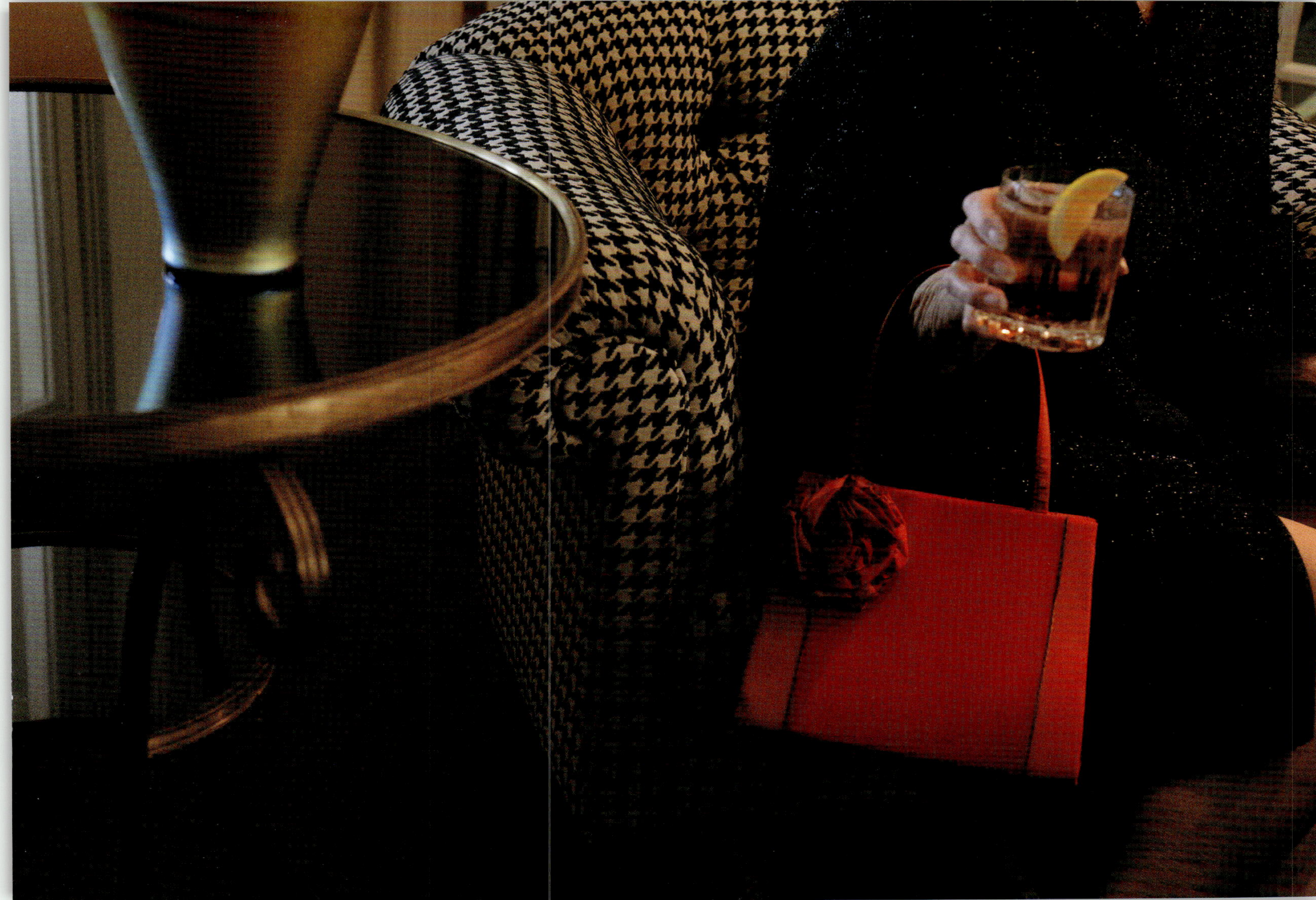

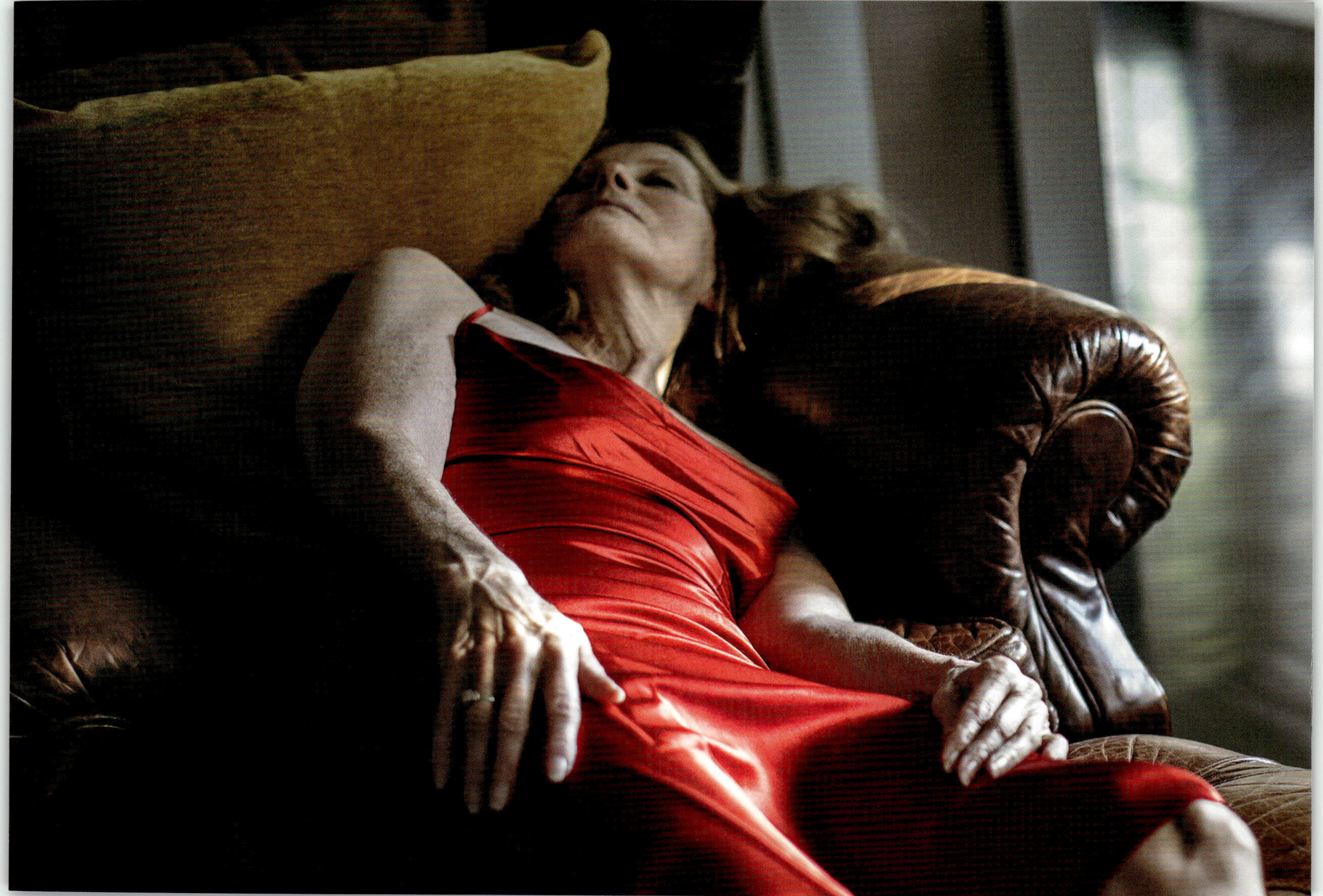

She wears Essie's
Lady in Red nail
polish. Red: the
universal color of
danger, strength,
passion, sexuality,
power, and courage.

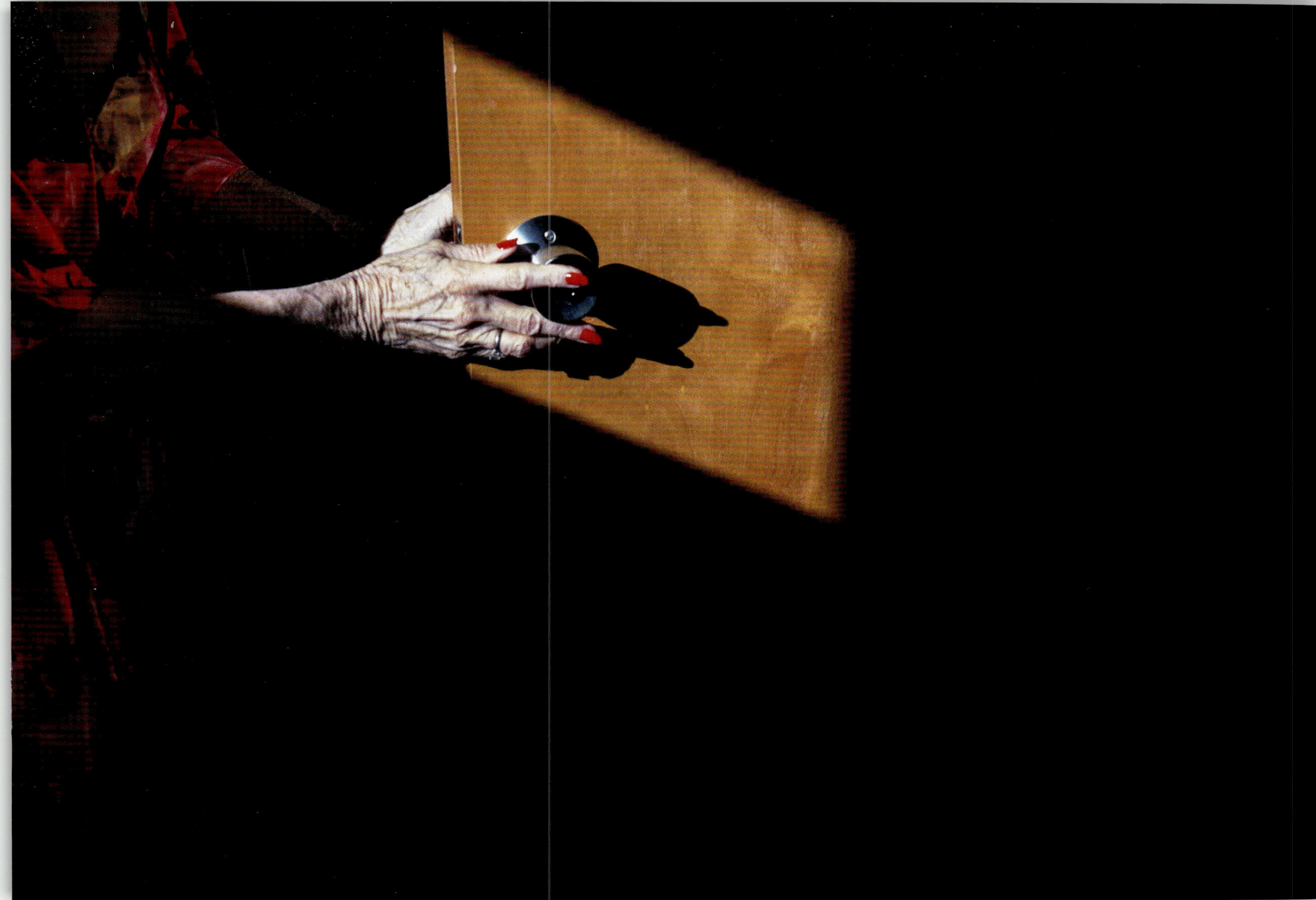

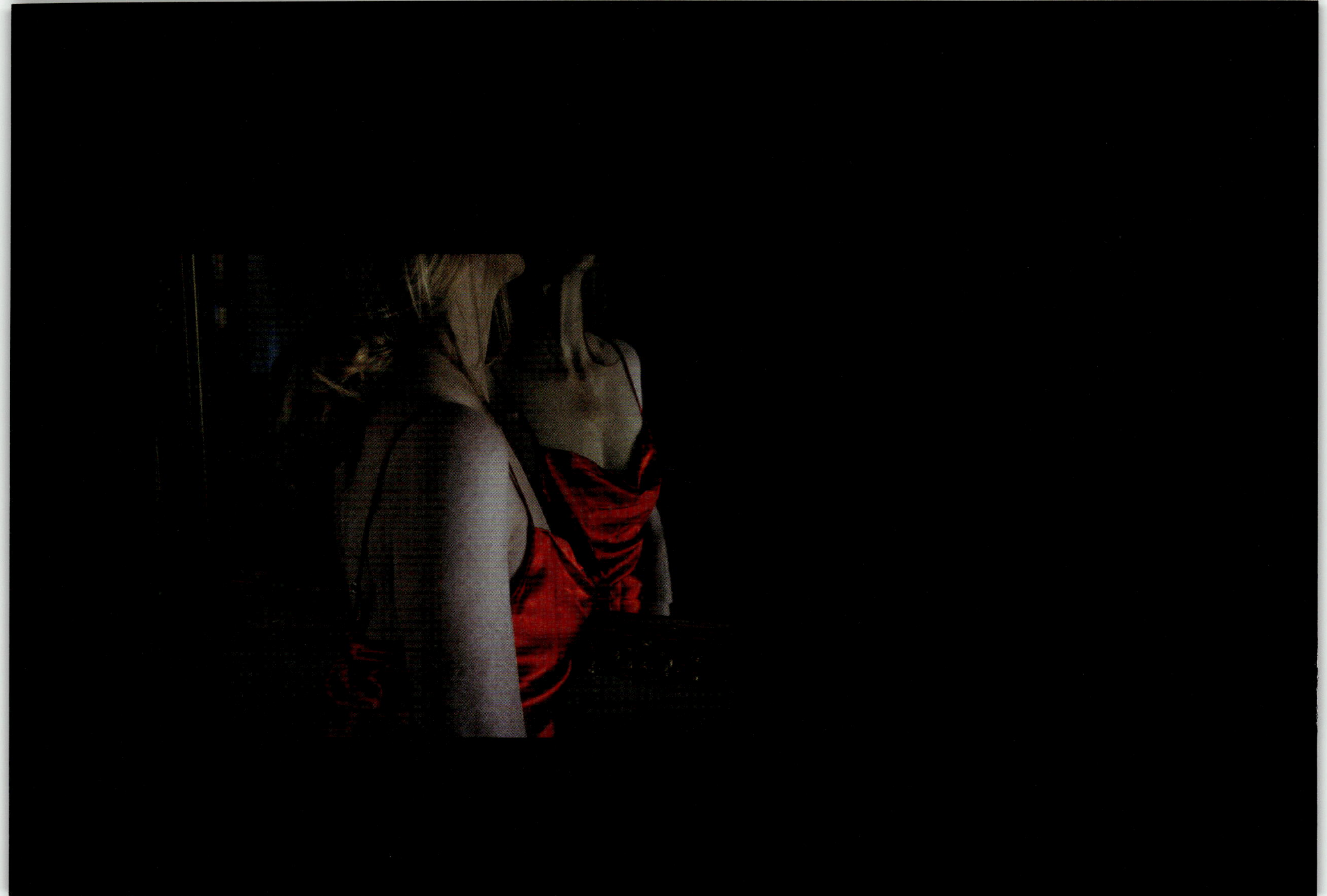

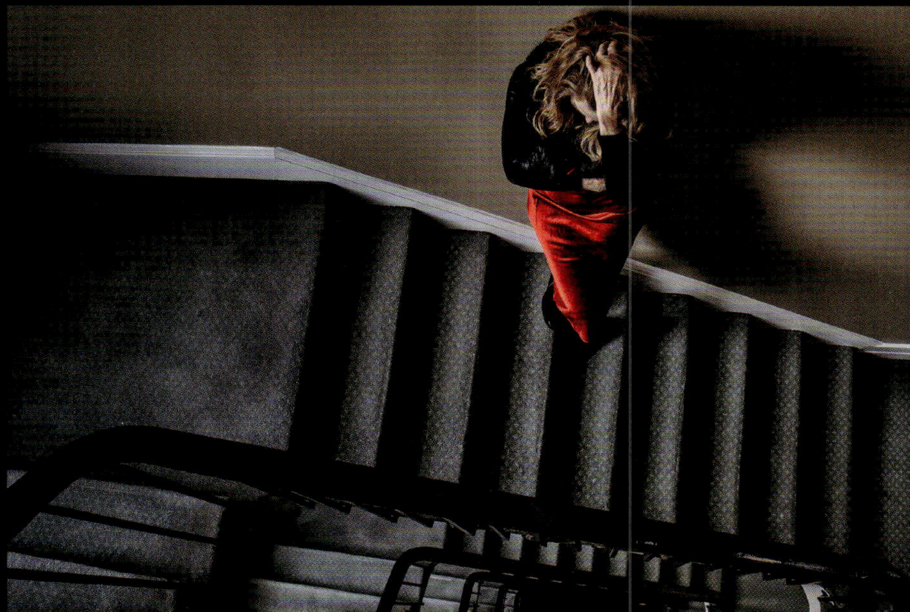

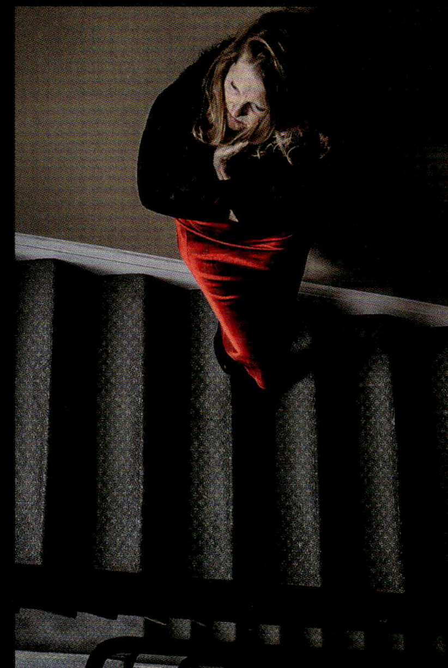

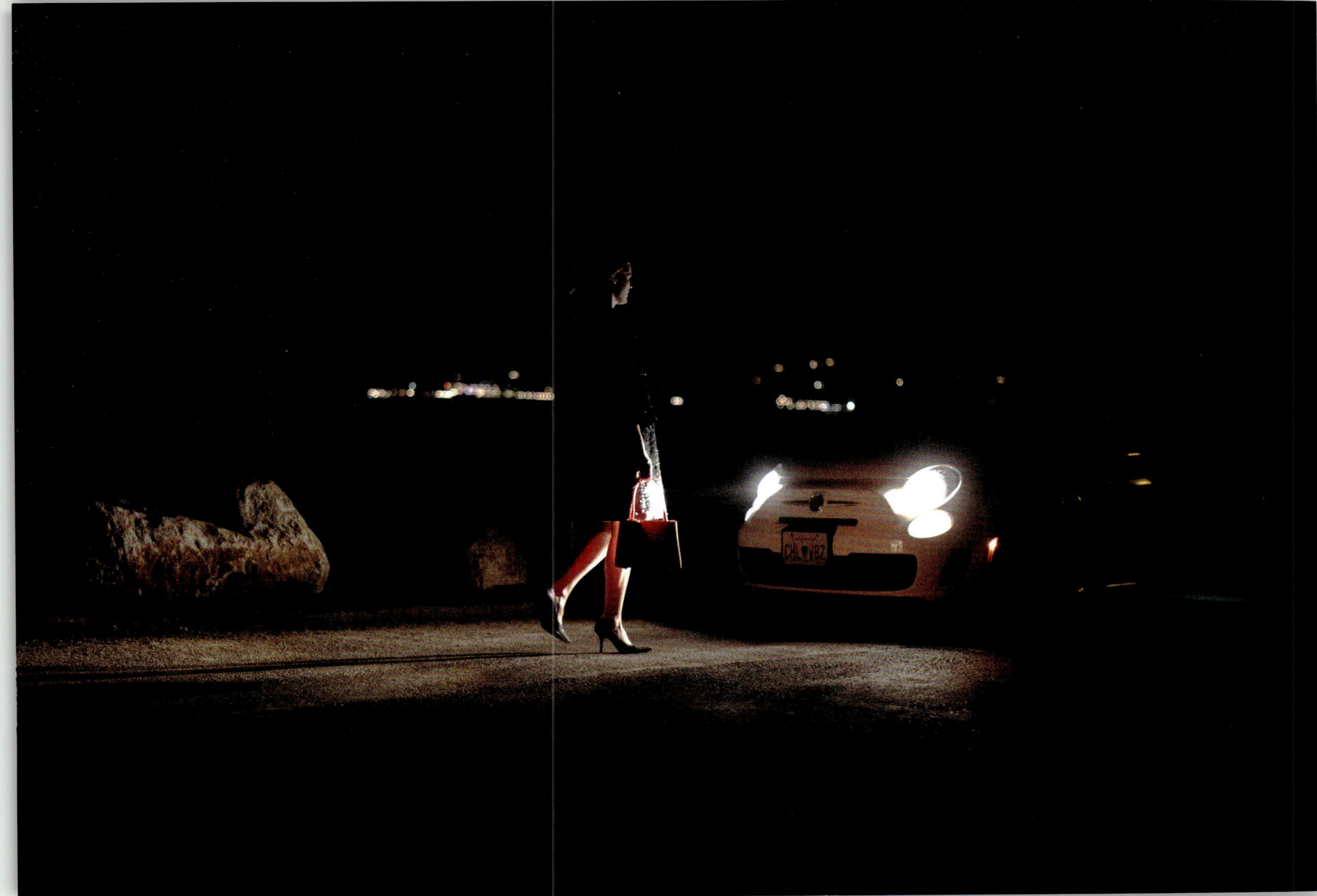

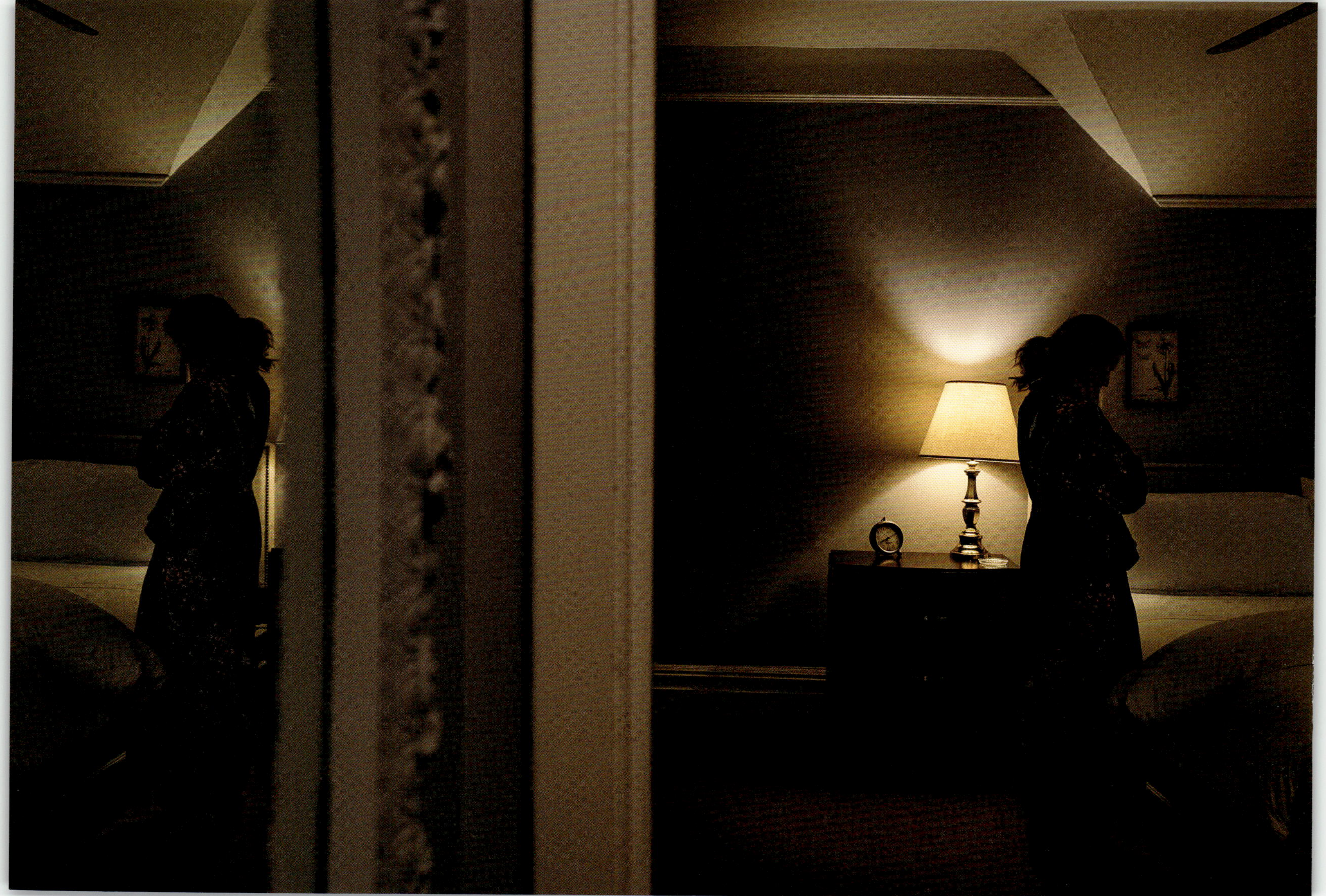

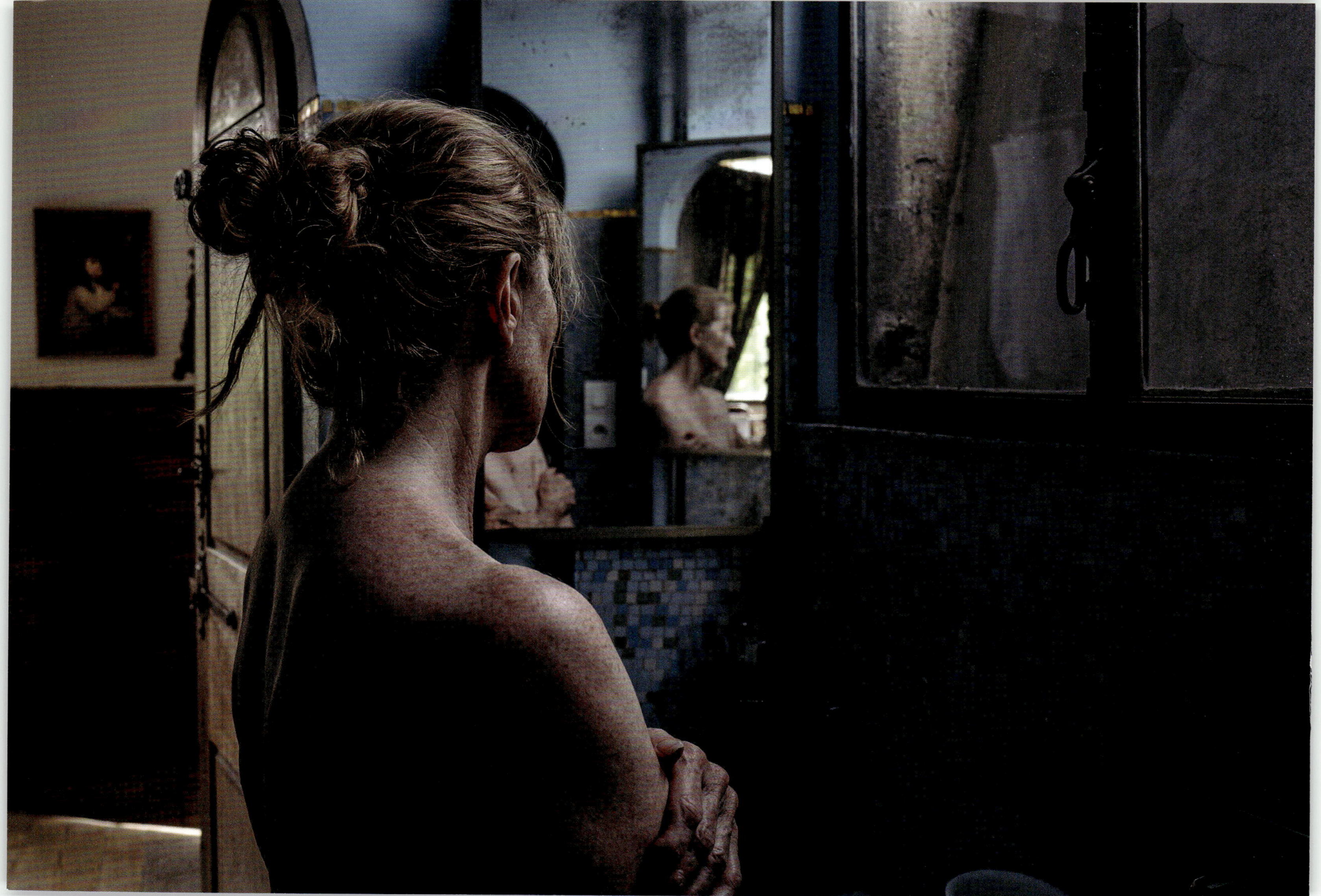

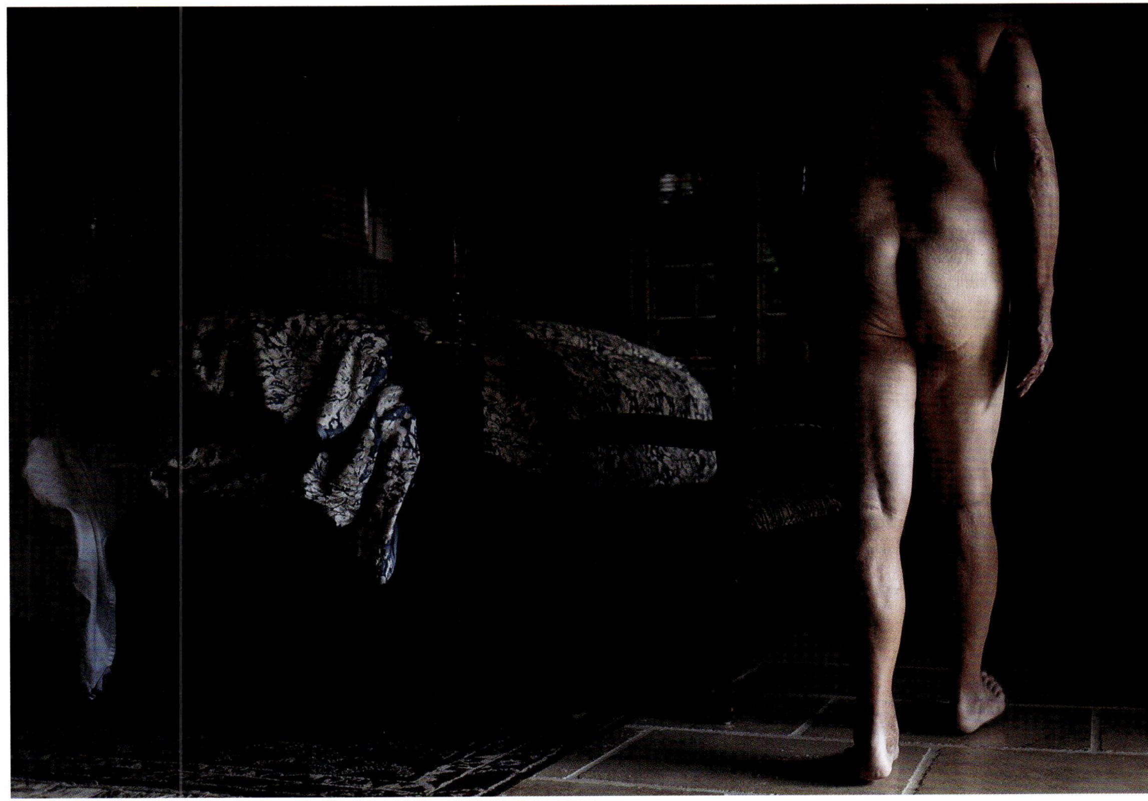

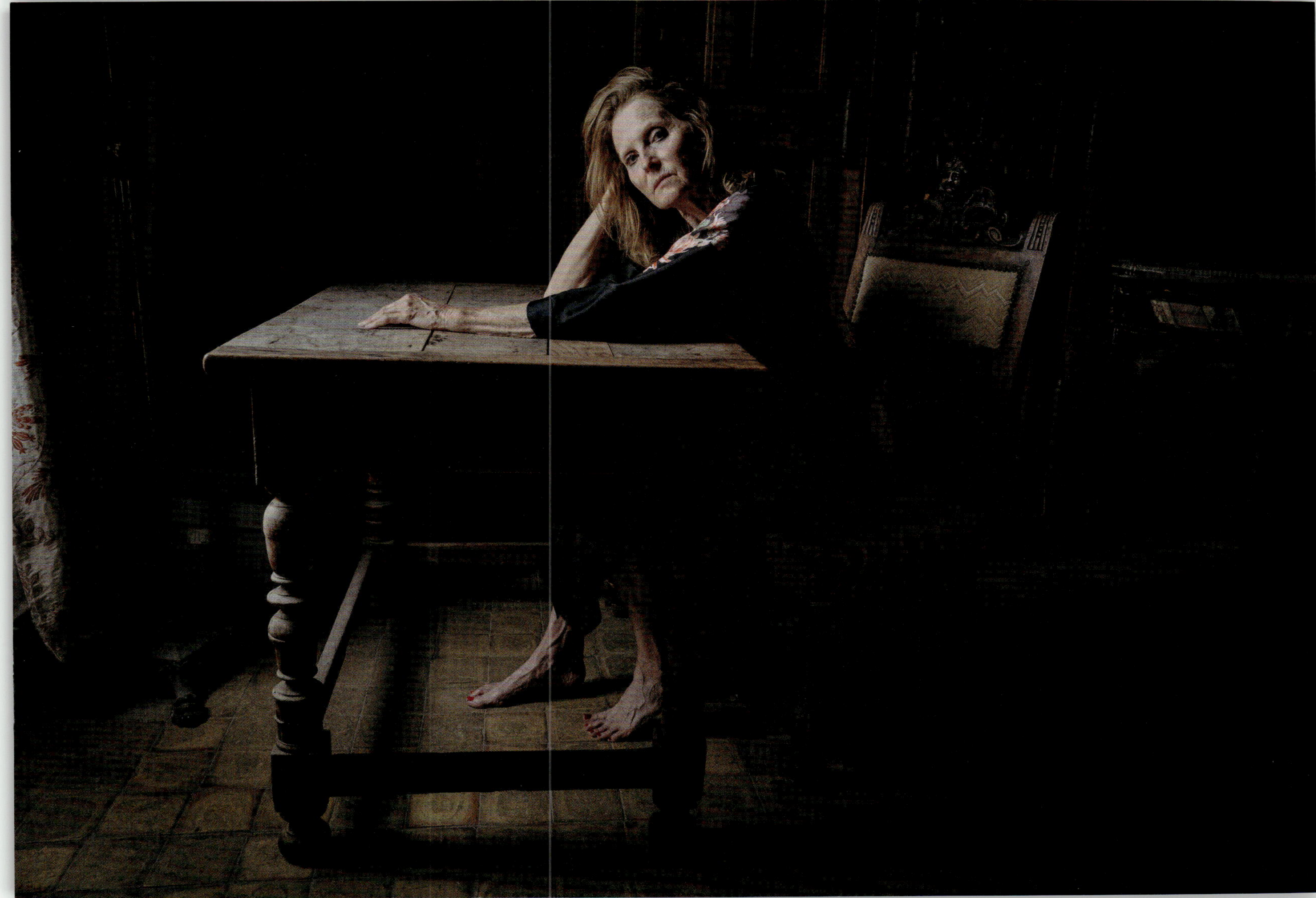

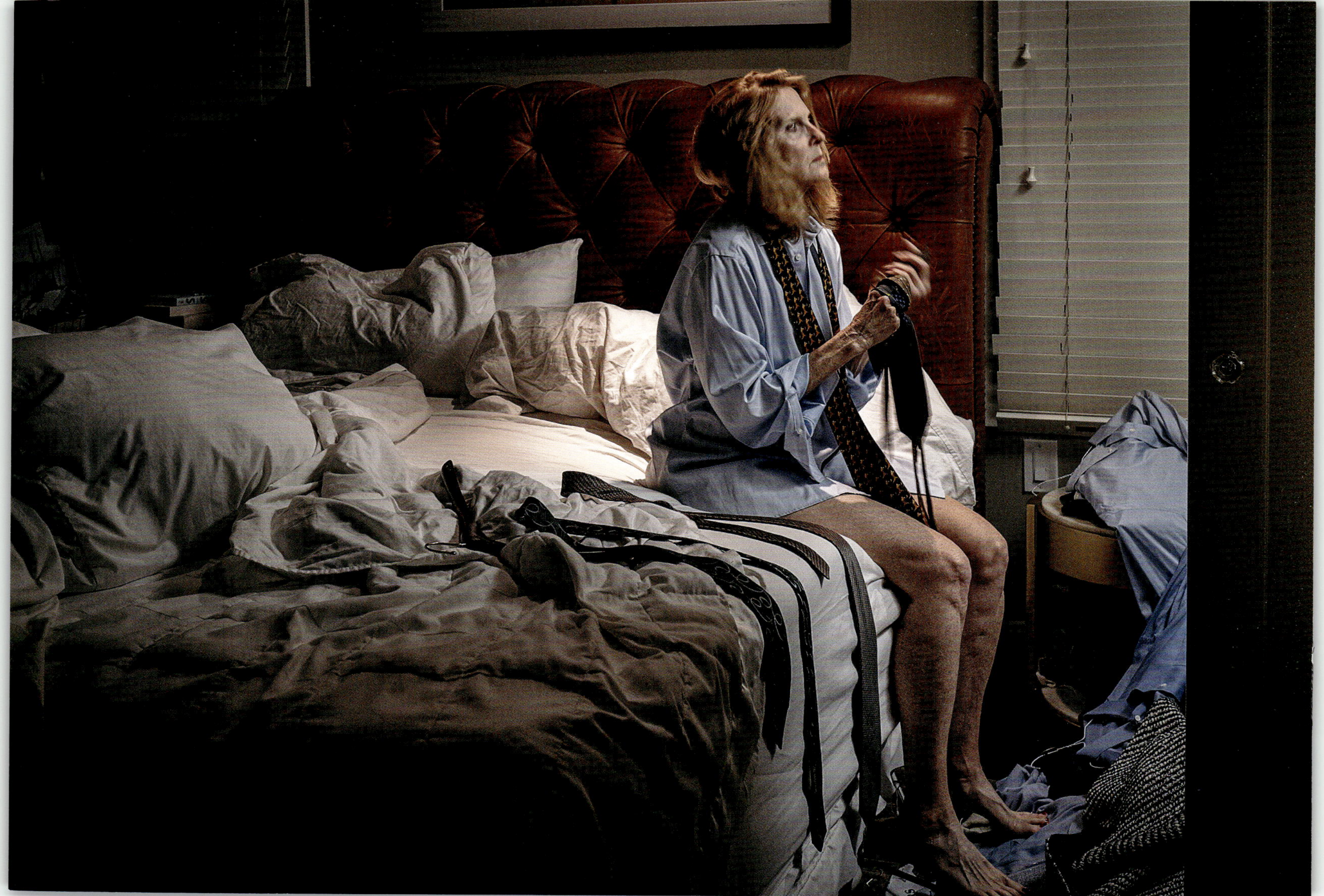

He leans in to kiss her good-night. She jumps back. She hasn't been kissed by another man in over twenty-five years. Later, alone in her bedroom, she hears a loud crack. The rod breaks, her husband's clothes spill to the ground. Is this a sign?

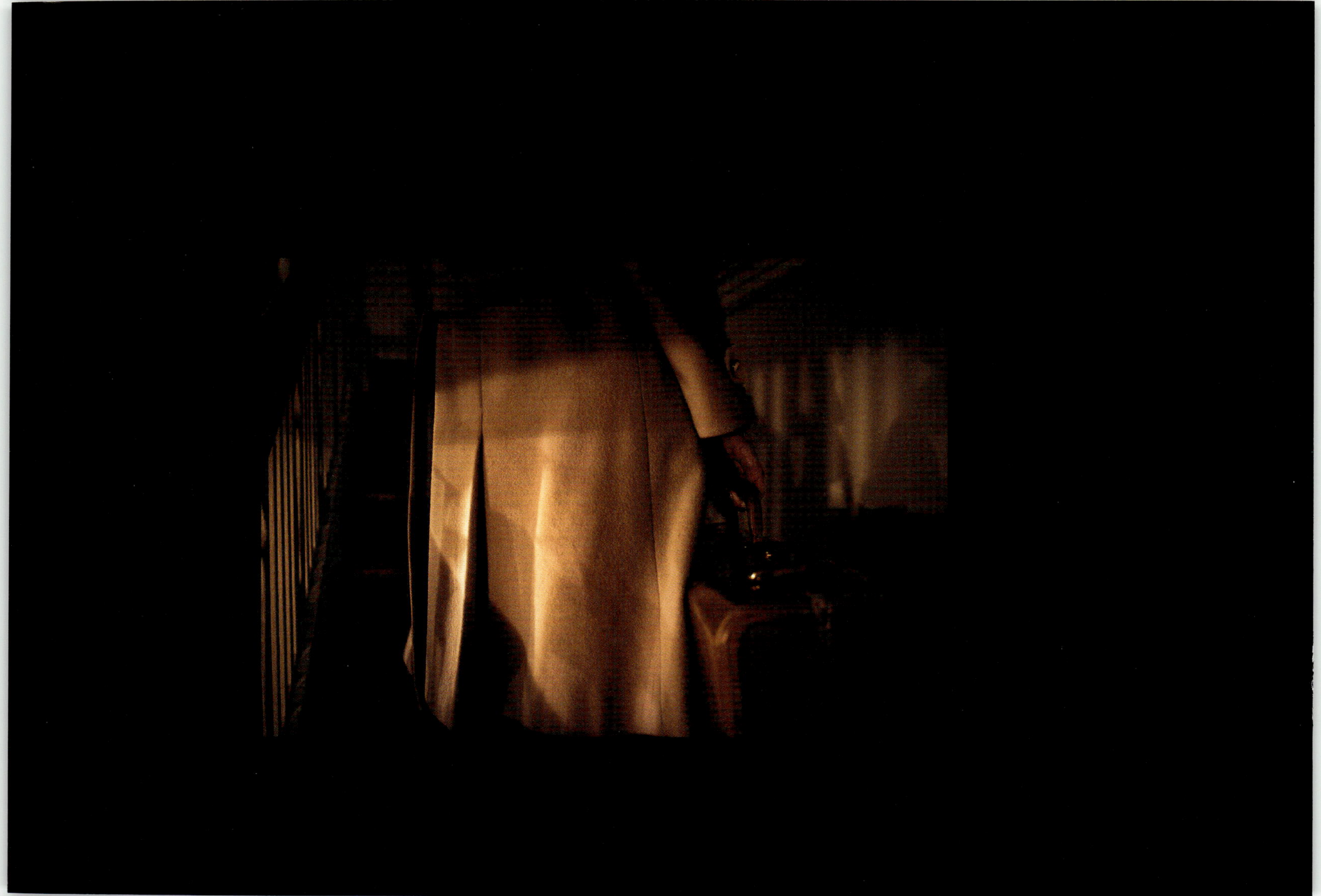

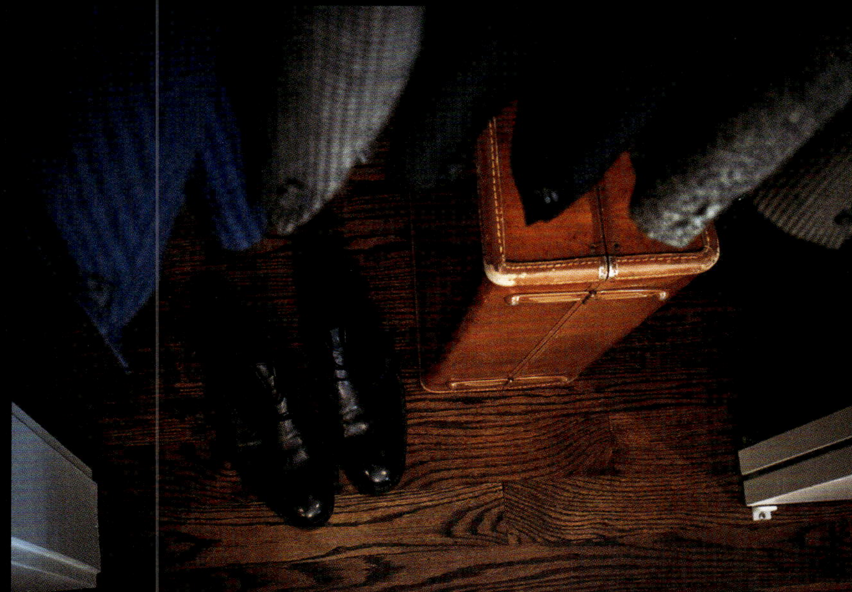

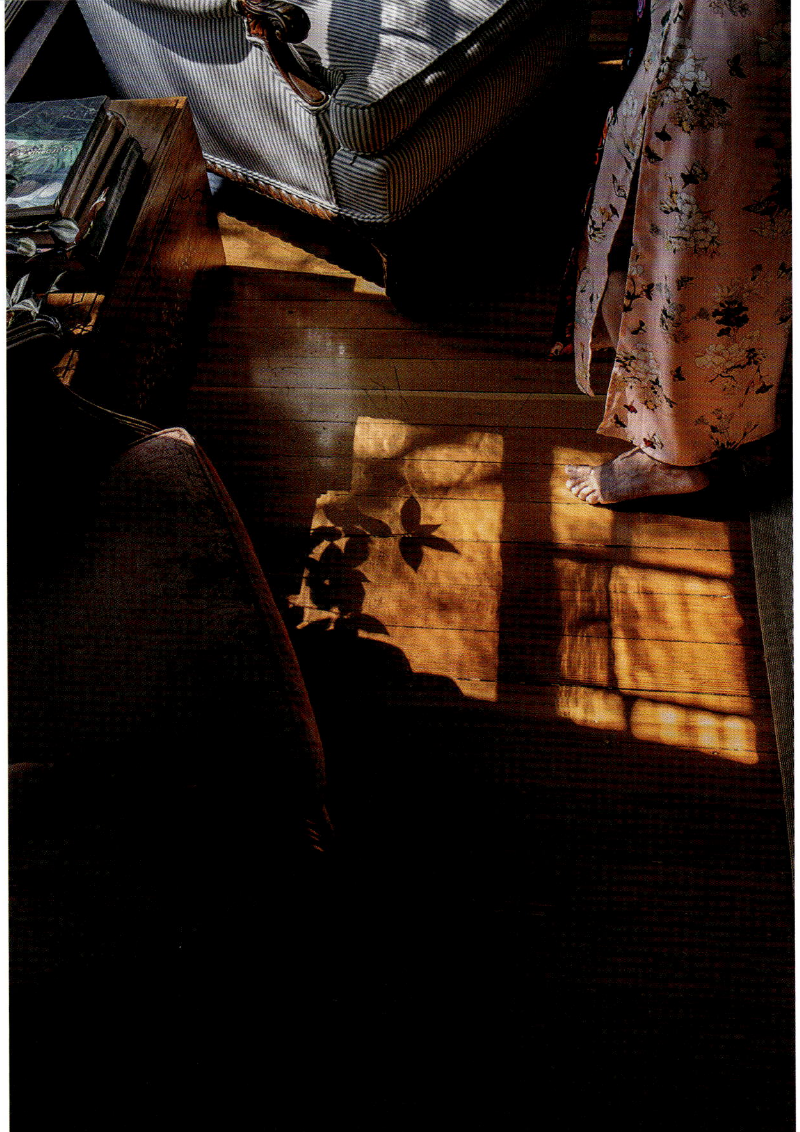

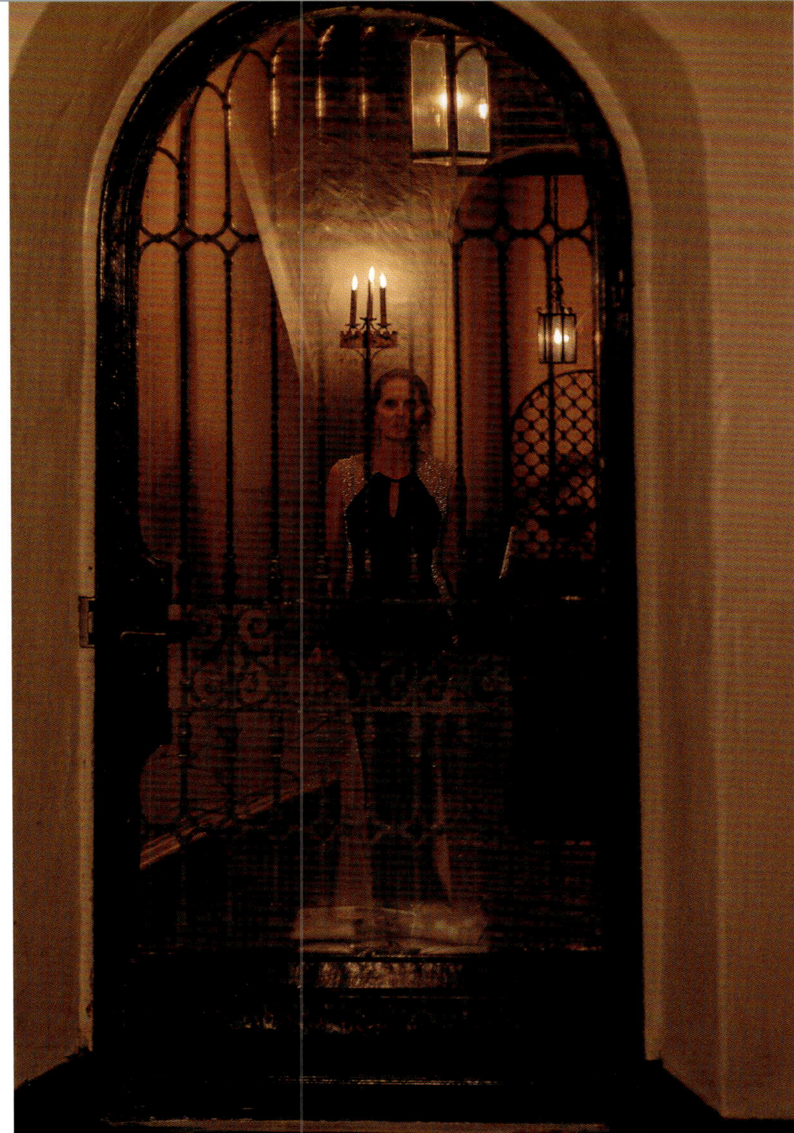

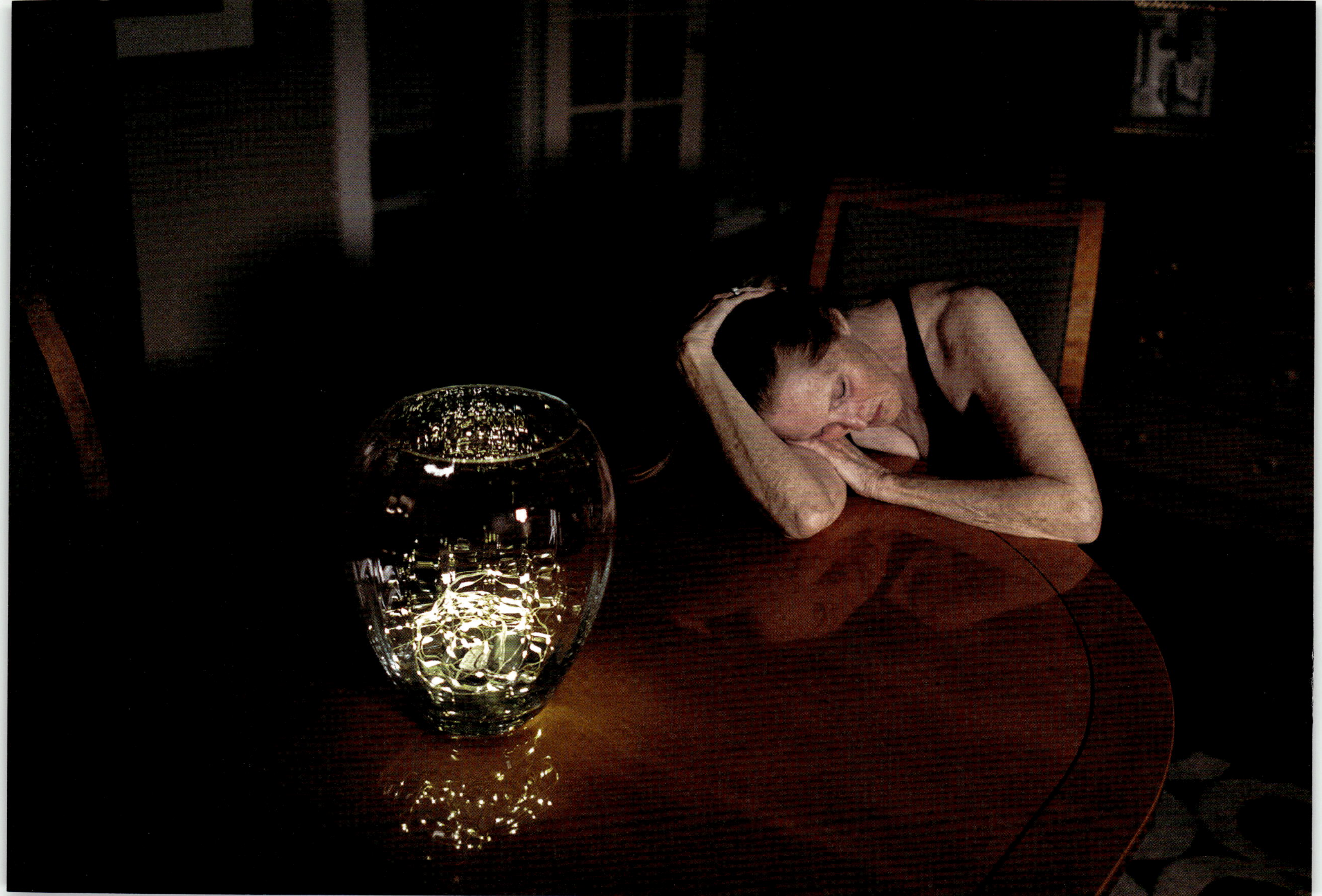

She wears dynasty-red silk pajamas, has unshaven legs, wears little makeup. Comfort and discomfort, nostalgic and unsettled, intimate and unnatural. A shift is happening.

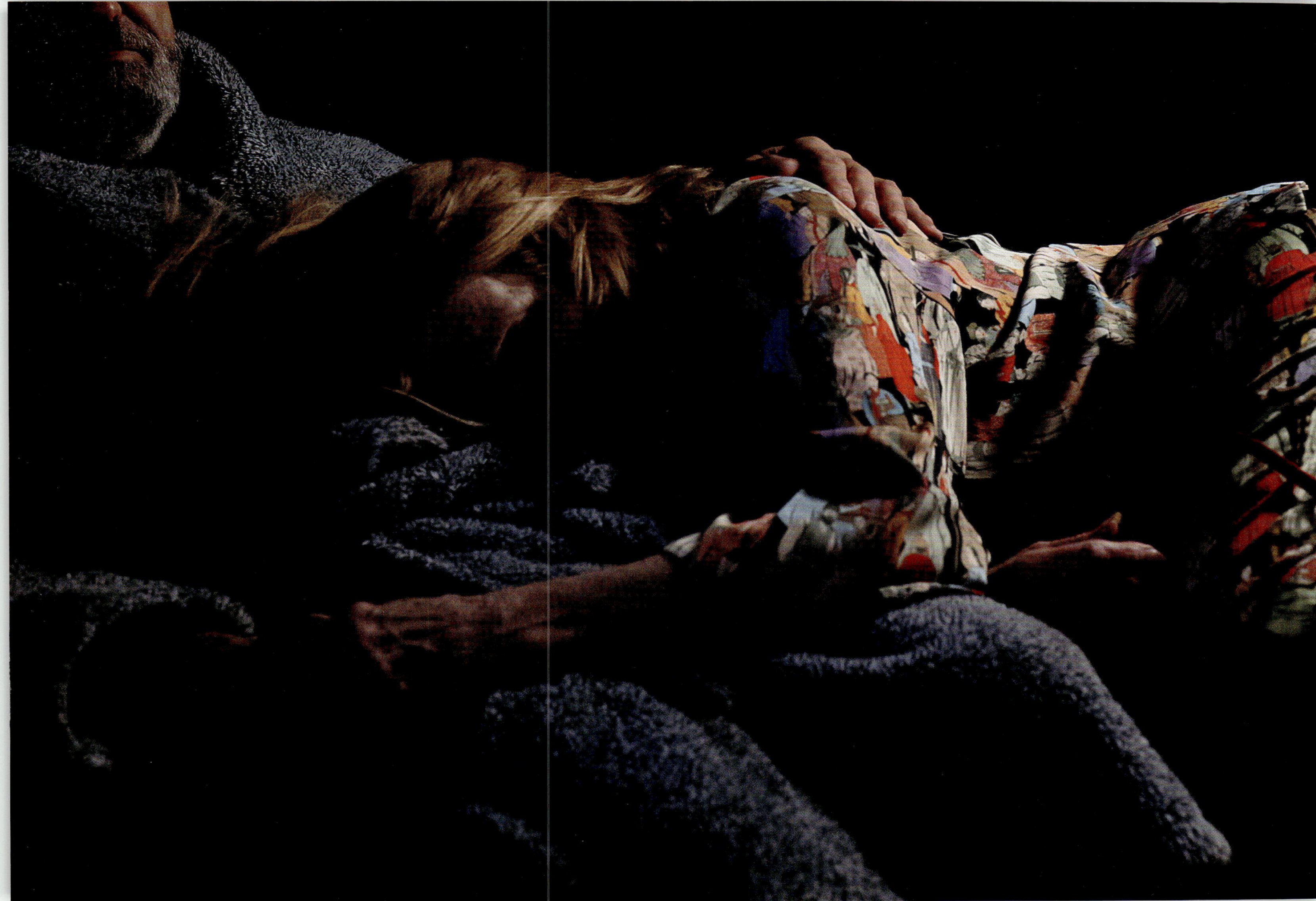

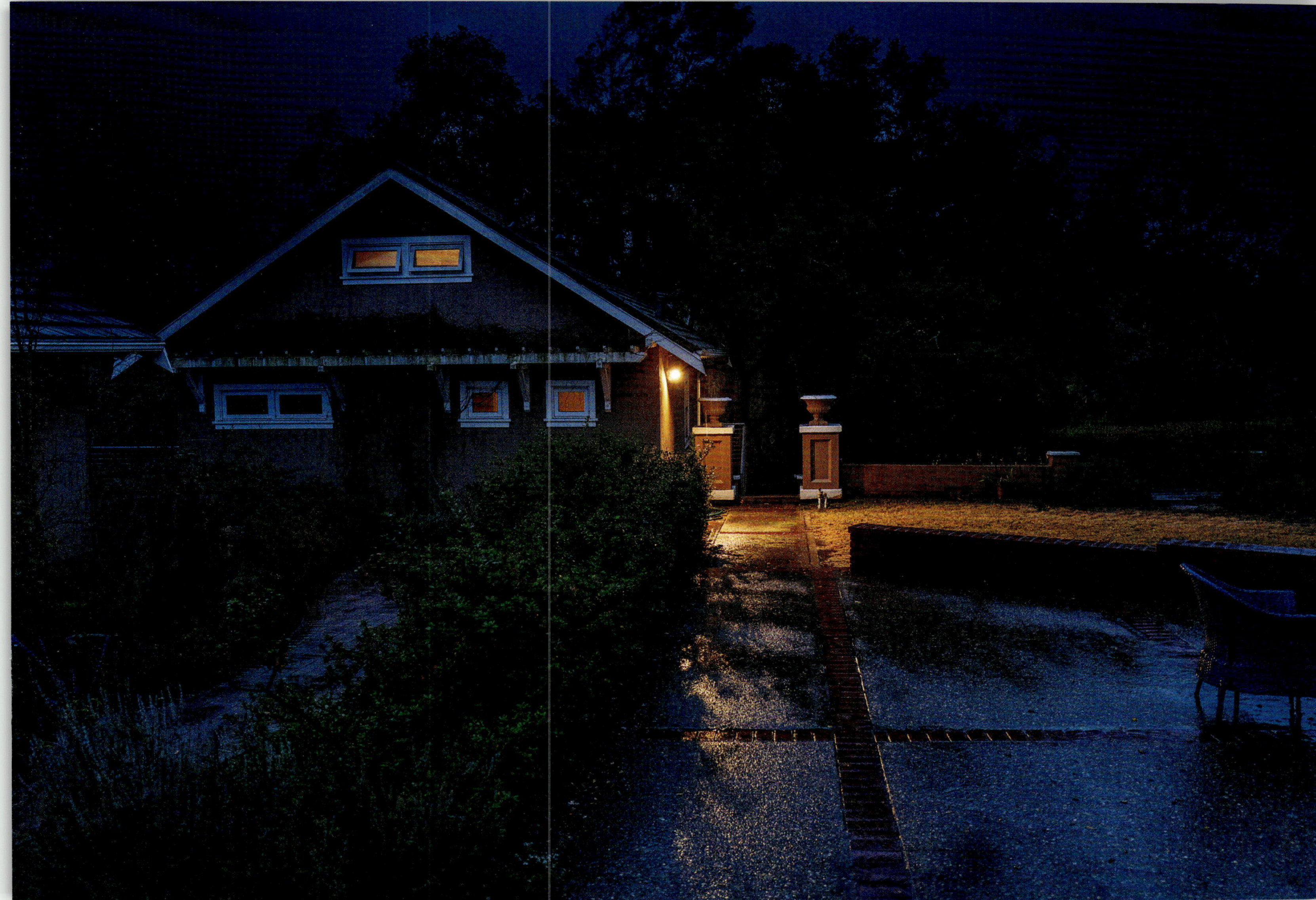

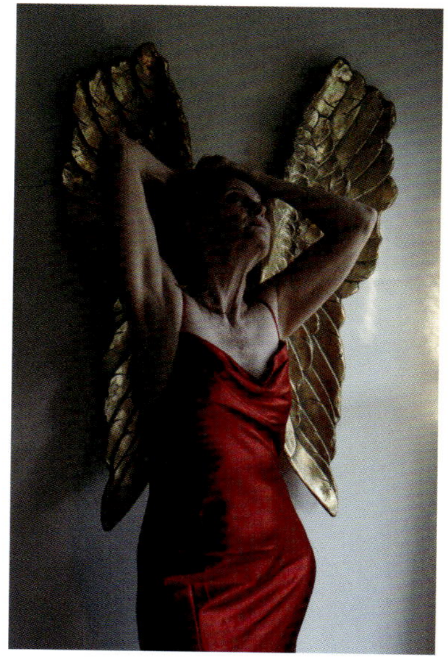

Conversation between Elinor Carucci and Jacque

JACQUE: Elinor, I remember when we first met in your workshop "The Experiences of Womanhood." I felt an immediate connection with you as a woman and as an artist. You provided a safe space for me to share my work and examine issues around sexuality, femininity, and change. Can you tell me a little bit about yourself as an artist and how you see our work relate?

ELINOR: I've been photographing myself and my family since I was fifteen, from an autobiographical standpoint. I'm from Israel; I came to the US in 1995, and I'm fifty-two now. You and I work in a different way, but we both work from autobiographical sources. We both try to bring honesty into our work and challenge the representation of women. I try to be universal in my theme, which you do as well.

JACQUE: This was the first project where I used myself as the subject; my first foray into self-portraiture. It began out of necessity during shelter in place at the beginning of the pandemic. I love to photograph people and the only people I had access to were myself and my partner. I quickly fell in love with the entire process because I realized I had more control; I could set up a scene, do things on my own time, and let things happen. I could be me, without trying to direct someone on how to pose, how to feel, etc. It felt so much more natural for me to act out my own story. At first, I admit, I felt it was a bit narcissistic and was embarrassed, but I quickly got over that. I learned I could use it to tell a much bigger, universal story. Elinor, why do you use yourself as the subject? Why self-portraiture?

ELINOR: I can go the deepest with myself. I can go to the most honest places. I can go in the wrong directions and then go back. I can hurt myself, I can expose myself, I can shame myself, so I think for me I am telling my story or other people's story through me. Also, because the access is infinite. You can go to all the parts of yourself more and more. It's a much bigger way to explore. You may or may not even use what you photograph—it's your call. There are no limits. For me, I can really tell the story in its fullest because it is my own. When I am thinking of writers, painters, and other creatives, they can explore the deepest parts of the character without having to use themselves because they don't need the actual person to be there. You can't find a person like this in our work. Like when I photographed my uterus, it had to be me. It would be very difficult with another person. In my mind it is so obvious it needs to be you in your work as well. I never questioned it. It was so natural. This is my answer to both of us. You can't tell your story using other people.

JACQUE: You see a lot of photography. What struck you about my work?

ELINOR: I was blown away by the quality of the work and the theme itself. The honesty in the sexuality, femininity, identity, and those types of feelings, surprised me, challenged me. Even being a feminist, liberal and open-minded, I was surprised by the conversations we had and are still having about women's issues: widowhood, ageism, sexuality, identity, and feminism. You challenged what it means to be a widow, to be sexual at an older age. I felt connected, inspired. I still remember the first day I saw your work. It was very thought-provoking.

JACQUE: It's interesting you talk about being surprised, because I surprised myself. I was a mom with two young boys. How could I possibly feel sexual? I was ashamed of those feelings, but you created an environment where I could start talking about it, learning from it. It was a real turning point for me. There were societal expectations about being a widow; a heaviness, a dark shroud, and an expectation that the more you sacrifice of yourself, the more loyal you are to your deceased husband. Feeling sexual scared the hell out of me. The project has helped me work through that, helped me to understand it. You helped tease this out of me.

ELINOR: As an artist, and even more importantly as a woman, you shouldn't be ashamed; you should be proud. You should push those elements in your work that allow for dealing with the shame, getting over the shame, and telling women about different aspects of who you are. Ignore societal norms, embarrassment; challenge it and inspire other women. Throw it the fuck out the window. It's kind of like what I did when I stopped dyeing my hair.

You are a widow. You want to be desired. You want to be with other men, which, by the way, has nothing to do with how much you loved your husband. I think there is a correlation: the better your relationship was with your husband, the more you want another connection. It's the opposite of what you would think.

JACQUE: I agree with that now. I think there was an inflection point, though, when I started feeling that, which allowed me to move forward in the art and explore my current feelings rather than focus on the guilt. I knew I wanted what I lost.

ELINOR: What is also interesting about your work as opposed to my work is that some of it is autobiographical and some of it is fictional. We discussed the importance of not letting your audience know which is which. Let them create the narrative they want in their head.

When you think about your audience, what do you think about?

JACQUE: Initially it was for other young widows. But the more I got into it, the more I realized I wanted it to be for anyone going through a major loss, and a major life-changing event, especially when one's identity has changed. And an untimely death is certainly a huge one. I wanted to create a platform, with new possibilities to allow for new conversations with people in a similar situation. When I went through it, there were very few resources. I felt so alone. There was nobody to talk to, only divorcees, and that was so different. There are more resources now.

We live in a time now when there are few rules. We can challenge the norms, and break the rules, which is both a blessing and a curse. I like to break the rules. I know you do as well. I wanted to create another option, a new definition of what it could look like to be a widow.

ELINOR: Maybe it was good there were no rules then. Maybe that is what pushed you to make this work; to have your voice heard and connect with other people. Maybe it provided the motivation. Be subtle about what is real and what is not real.

JACQUE: It did help me later to reach out to other women and have those conversations. And looking at the images I created; being honest and asking questions. The sexuality scared me, shocked me. But why?

ELINOR: There is always an element of surprise when we look at our pictures, even though we're the ones taking them. We see more when we photograph. And even more when we photograph ourselves. When we put the camera as a mirror in front of our eyes, even more, there is a process of self-discovery. Do you even remember the first picture?

JACQUE: Yes, it was the one on the cover of the book, with me walking by my armoire with the purse. I was fascinated with the purse, womanhood, and femininity. And I was just beginning to play with self-portraiture. I learned as I had to articulate it. It was an organic experience.

ELINOR: Your work uses so many metaphors: the use of the color red, the purse, portals, the noir feel. And then it became more fictional. Why?

JACQUE: The metaphors were important but organic; objects and situations that I was attracted to. I learned so much more about their importance later as I was looking back on the work. How fitting they were for the project. The fiction was very intentional. It gave me a sense of anonymity. It allowed me to both reenact and create a new scene to tell my story. It was so much easier to show the world a more controversial or sexual scene when it wasn't me.

Also, I have always been fascinated with the moving image, so it felt natural to take it in that direction—a film noir. Edgy, with the femme fatale, a strong woman taking risks. It gave me another safe place to play in, to tell my story. It's a fictional character. It's not me. I don't want the viewer to know which is which.

ELINOR: We talked about some of our idols, usually movie stars, and how they are portrayed, how they become a part of us, especially when we were younger. Michelle Pfeiffer and Diane Lane were a couple of mine. I saw them at an age when they could help define who I am. The movie stars we grow up with are very important to our identity as a woman. It's not you but it is you. It adds a legitimacy to be something.

JACQUE: I totally agree. I was attracted to similar idols, but in this project Marilyn Monroe became very important. I could relate to her experiencing an untimely death—even though it was my husband who died, it was still a tragedy. She's a strong female, sexy, independent…it was something I had to explore. I was fascinated with her at the time; I read books (like *Blonde*) and watched movies about her. I even went to see where she died in Brentwood, California.

It's interesting, now that I am aging, I am searching for a new role model. But I don't see that person now. Maybe it is Diane Keaton. This may be a catalyst for my next project.

ELINOR: Fashion is another part of your story; it brought something else out of you. Jacque, it was important if you would choose this dress, high heels, this wig. I was selfishly thinking it's "fun time" and looked forward to your next set of images to see what you would bring into the work. The props, the settings, the emotions were all very deliberate and different. We all alter the way we present ourselves; it allows us to do something else, to be someone else, gives us the permission to be something different—a wig, a mask, etc.—to get to other sides of you that you didn't even know were there. I'm always excited to see what you are bringing into your work. You bring different elements into your work, even if it is something like flowers, which is very inspiring, and it affects each of us in different ways.

JACQUE: Most definitely. It was all a very deliberate part of telling my story. It allowed me to immerse myself in both the real and imagined part of the script. I had so much fun finding the clothes, the props, and the settings.

ELINOR: I also love the performance part of your work. When I was thinking of artists today, I was thinking about Jess Dugan, who is a nonconforming gender and challenges our way of thinking about gender and women. And Cindy Sherman, and Claude Cahun, a French surrealist born in the late nineteenth century and a feminist who challenges the way people think about sexuality, and gender with women, and has a lot of performance in her work—and all the way to Nikki S. Lee and using performance to understand who she is as an immigrant. A lot of artists are using performance today.

Your work is somewhere in between these genres, working more from an autobiographical perspective and using performance. Your work is in between mine and Jess Dugan's and the performance artists'. It's important for you to keep some of the mystery. The decisions we make as artists are way beyond how we take the image; it's what we want to say as an artist. How we edit, title, process, etc. All those decisions added to the creation of *The Red Purse*.

JACQUE: Yes, the mystery is very important to me. And I felt I had to perform to tell my story. Another artist that inspired me was Jennifer McClure and her project *You Who Never Arrived*.

ELINOR: First you only photographed you, but then after a year you started showing men. Why?

JACQUE: It started off as an exploration of myself using self-portraiture, but then I felt like it was important to bring in other characters to tell the story. It was difficult at first for me to include men. First, I just showed their backs, profiles, like with David, my partner. Then, in the middle, it became very fictional, as if I was running around like Marilyn, taking risks, exploring. I was a different person now looking for a partner—in my forties versus last time when I was in my twenties. I knew I had different choices now than when I was in my twenties. I didn't want to replicate what I had with my husband. I wanted that to stay sacred. Then, towards the end of the project, I began getting more comfortable showing more of David, and in a more natural way. You helped me get more comfortable with the sexual part of the work. To be brave. I think you come from a culture, in Israel, where you can be more open about sexuality and your body. Much more so than here in the US. And especially with older people.

ELINOR: And we even talked about, Is David dangerous for the project? At first, I was happy for you. But OMG, I thought, Will this new relationship kill the wild, subversive, exciting Jacque? The friendship, the commitment? I was nervous about what's going to happen to the project. We also discussed whether you would keep the fictional characters. Or would you change the project? And how would the story end?

JACQUE: We discussed the story arc—initially just photographing myself, then very hesitantly including a man, David, showing no faces, because this was safe. Then moving forward suggesting there were other men, other relationships, then ending with more of David…showing a kind of sensitive sexuality and contentment. It never gets fully resolved. I get more comfortable with it. It slowly begins to feel like a new normal.

It was important that it not end feeling like it was all wrapped up in a bow. I didn't want to impose my ending and/or story on others viewing the work. The world always wants a happy ending. I believe there are many options, and they can all be OK.

I am a happy person. And I am still a strong, independent woman breaking barriers. I don't want people to feel like I have stepped away from that. It is still a very important part of my identity. I don't want to lose that. I learned both parts of my life can coexist.

ELINOR: The feminist statement is important to you. Why?

JACQUE: It is who I am. It is who you are. I think we both try to create new role models, just like we had to in the past, to help other people. My dream is for this book to add to that narrative. It is the feminist narrative, and I am proud of that.

ELINOR: *The Red Purse* is not just about being a widow; it's about sexuality and identity and challenging the norms, especially beyond a certain age. It is much bigger, much more universal. Did you start out with this in mind?

JACQUE: No, it morphed into that. Ageism began to take on a bigger role because I have aged. My camera took me there.

Widowhood was the catalyst, but it goes beyond that. As a child, I never saw my parents being sexual. We don't typically see older people being sexual. It's just starting to surface on the Hollywood screens.

ELINOR: That's crazy, because they say the groups that are having more sex now are those in their seventies. We are sexual beings. This is why your work is so important. We're feeling shame and embarrassment about older sex. You offer another view.

JACQUE: Some people see or hear about the work and are shocked and don't know what to do with it. Especially my children, at first. But I get that—we don't want to think about our parents being sexual beings. I know I didn't.

ELINOR: Being a mother and a widow, how did you handle it? How did you handle the dating back then, and how will you handle the book today? Two very different scenarios.

JACQUE: At the time, I hid it. I went undercover and separated it from my children. Maybe I still do. I wouldn't hold David's hand in front of them. I still don't. Maybe subconsciously I feel as if I am betraying my husband. Which I know makes no sense at all. When I showed them the images initially, they tended to shy away and didn't want to see the work. They are proud that I am being recognized, but they really didn't want to talk about it. But now, a couple of years later, they are both married, and in love; they are warming up to it. But I'm sure they secretly wish I was publishing my work about my exotic travels and/or street photography. I have boys. I don't know if it would be any different with daughters.

I still call Ed my husband. I have kids. He is their father. And I struggle with what to call my new partner, David, still, after almost twenty years.

ELINOR: You seemed to have used photography to become more comfortable with who you became. To create a persona, you had to become one, to find the outfits, the expressions, etc. It had to be real. I think you wouldn't have become who you are today without being a photographer, an artist, without confronting it.

JACQUE: I agree. It takes a lot of internal work to create the images. It also requires a lot of vulnerability to see yourself through the lens. But I also get to make a lot of choices on what goes into the project. Many of the outtakes aren't pretty. I have the power to select what I want to show. But I want to be honest. I want to tell the story. It's a balance. Does this happen to you as well?

ELINOR: Yes, of course it does. Especially when it comes to the topic of ageism. It's a struggle, because I'm trying to make a strong body of work that is very real, telling who I am. It's tempting to just choose the beautiful images, to retouch, etc., but I have a responsibility to my audience to be authentic, to be honest. Did you see my post last year about when I did lip fillers? It got so much attention.

Wanda Sykes uses humor to do this. You need to seduce the viewers, and many times we do this with beauty. We need to find the balance between bringing in the beauty and bringing in the hard truth. And the reality and the complicated truth of the beauty and the horrors and challenges and joys. How do we find the balance without sugarcoating it, or romanticizing it? But also, because then it is not relatable. [We] want to create what's relatable, and something that is beautiful.

JACQUE: I got braver as I was photographing later in the project, like the woman in the pink coat in Room 24. Allowing for the quirky, less pretty. I see now that I brought the wig in to help me do this. It was safer. See, I am learning again as I talk to you. Even as I look at my images now from a couple of years ago, I see that I was thinner, had less wrinkles, etc. I see the changes. The camera creates a time stamp. I'm sure you see this as well.

ELINOR: Most definitely. And it seems more challenging to women. Women are more self-conscious because of how our society is judging us. We're always challenged when we see ourselves. Sometimes, there is a gap in how we see ourselves inside and how the world sees us. This is the cruelty of our bodies and age. Yet we are who we are. We want to have sexuality, adventures, dreams...yet our appearance continues to change. It's why our work is so important as artists. It can help us get used to what we really look like. It closes the gap, to see who we are now. Maybe it is hard for us, it's indoctrinated in us: we always hear we must be beautiful and young to be sexual. That is why I think representation is so important.

We are sexual beings, we want to celebrate life, have adventures. It's true for all of us, beyond just widows, which is why representation is so important. And our work helps this. Maybe if I saw women with gray hair in their pubic hairs in *Playboy*, I would feel different. You see it in the fine-art culture much more so than in the commercial world. We're dealing with the challenges of reality, and many times the commercial world will follow. And when it becomes cool, maybe even Hollywood will follow. Hopefully we will help bring on that change.

The work we are doing, and the kind of honesty, is much easier to do in fine art versus the commercial world. It's much less about the financial bottom line. There is less at stake. We can take bigger risks.

JACQUE: You brought up something very important—that the work can strike people differently at different times, at different ages, from different angles, etc. Especially when people are ready for it.

ELINOR: That is why I asked you about your audience. For me, my audience is everyone. Anyone that is interested in life. It's the truth I want to bring about in my work. We are talking about life—our dreams—and our audience is everybody. Men, women, old, young, divorced, widowed, single. Bring truth to the work. One of our goals is to challenge people's thinking, to make people upset, so maybe later it triggers something. I had a guy that saw my *MOTHER* series, and the post-C-section image, the nursing bra image, and other more honest images years ago. He didn't like it then but more recently he told me these images helped him later, after his wife had a child. Often, we connect with people at different times.

JACQUE: I agree. Which is why we do the work. And my truth is about challenging the norms that involve life-changing events, even death—which we all experience. It is life.

ELINOR: It's universal; it connects us with people when they are going through something similar. It's then that we remember; it's then that we connect. It's like how we remember the song, the movie, etc. It helps us. It may come later.

JACQUE: One last question. I could talk to you for hours on end. But is there an image that stands out to you, and why?

ELINOR: Yes, of course. The one in the dining room, with you drinking wine; there is a man there and another woman. It talks about you in the context of being in a bar, restaurant, a nice place, and there is a woman in the background. So many stories, so many questions. Maybe it is how we were brought up; there is the blond, the sexual being, the Marilyn, and the woman in the background with dark hair watching but not watching. There is so much mystery and ambiguity.

JACQUE: Thank you again so much. It was so good to share our stories, our feelings, and our adventures. I have so much respect for you as an artist and as a person. I appreciate your straightforward approach, your candor. I always learn so much from you; just as I did today.

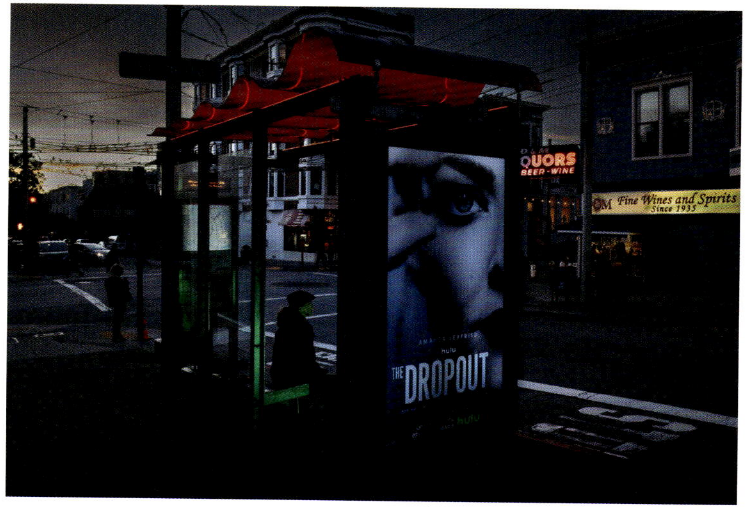
QUORS
BEER-WINE
Fine Wines and Spirits
Since 1935
THE DROPOUT

Afterword I

Our central figure is pictured sitting at a table that is draped with a white tablecloth. Dressed in black, she sips reluctantly at a glass of red wine. She appears preoccupied, deep in thought, unhappy. Around her are several people engaged in their own worlds. A man wearing a baseball cap also sits at the table drinking wine. Our lead character is not interested in him. Nor is she paying attention to the woman at her left drinking alone, facing a mirror. There is a wrapped gift on a chair, with a note attached, but it holds no attraction. For whom is this gift? Why are these people gathered? Is this a restaurant? A wine tasting? If so, it is a sad and unpopular one. I look out the window, down to the street. There is an older woman in a white hat, hunched over, pulling a handcart with a large cardboard box. Our redheaded protagonist isn't drawn to any of these people or options, yet she somehow knows they exist. The only thing on the table is wine. I let my mind wander and imagine the table as a white-draped casket. This is a wake, and our lead is about to snap.

The Red Purse is about what happens next. Through a series of photographic tableaux, photographer Jacque Rupp poses a series of "what if" questions about the choices she made or could have made after the passing of her husband. These are not pictures about grief. *The Red Purse* is about renewal, perseverance, and harnessing the power of desire to carve a new path after the loss of a life partner. It is about giving permission to rediscover oneself, try on different personae, and beginning anew.

Images of the red purse appear in several of the photographs, but it's a ruse. Rupp doesn't actually need the purse. It's the metaphor she uses to awaken her own power. The images are somewhere between somberness and play.

Cloaked in many of the hallmarks of noir, Rupp's photographs suggest but avoid the brazenness of violence and instead explore the noir's heart—passion. Passion that often begins in the underground and darkness. The majority of Rupp's photographs were made at night—they are bathed in black, the unknown.

I would imagine the internal dialogue of a widow is filled with questions like "Now what?" "How do I start over again when the person with whom I built my life is gone?" Life and the world must feel like a distortion of their usual, reliable forms, light itself choked with haze. But for many like me, the darkness is where we must go to do our best thinking and feeling. It is when I am alone in the dark that I notice the first sparks of life, the glimmers of light. It is where I notice that death and life are two sides of the same coin. They come from the same place. Eros and Thanatos, the gods of love and death, are always engaged in a dance. We cannot have one without the other. They are fundamental drives that propel us forward. *The Red Purse* is a metaphor for this perpetual cycle and shows us that according to the Buddhists, we humans live in the realm of desire. It's what makes us come back again and again and be reborn. Through giving life to her children and continuing to live and continue through the death of her husband, Rupp chooses to live life through passion, play, and risk-taking.

Throughout the series, we see Rupp move from fear toward rediscovering self. She tries on several new faces, but none of them stick. They're all red herrings. Through the photographs we witness her bumps in the road, her insecurities, her flirtations with paths that turn out to be wrong for her. Not religion, not alcohol, not acting younger than her actual age, not her flirtations with men. None of them work. What she is left with is herself, her own predicament at her stage in life. Our protagonist harnesses the power of the erotic impulse to explore life's possibilities and explore people she could possibly become. For her this is the only way. The other choices were too easy. Our redheaded protagonist is carving her own path and we don't know where it's going to lead. As with the best tales, in the end we are left with ambiguity. Many noir stories are crimes of passion that end in devastation. The ending of *The Red Purse* is not yet written. This is partly what makes it so compelling. It is a precarious, erotic story, with darkness and delight, and I can't wait to see what happens next.

—Jason Langer, 2023

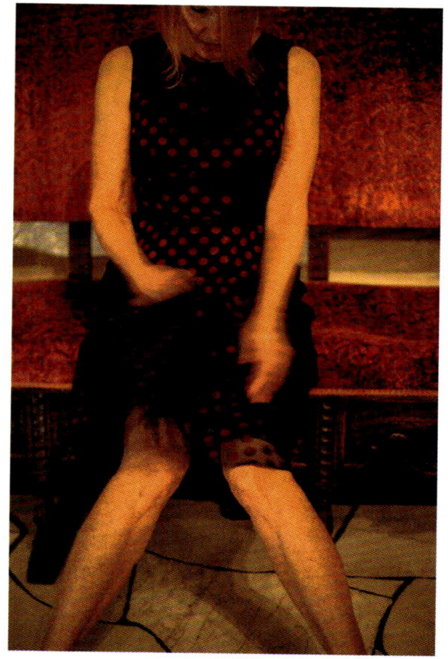

Afterword II

I remember the first time the red purse made an appearance in a photograph. It seemed tame compared to the lace undergarment worn by the woman carrying it. I would follow this character for years, the mysterious woman, through visits to hotels and bars and restaurants, to choices made, choices embraced, choices regretted. I would watch her dressing, undressing, high heels poised to take her to her next destination, lipstick applied and reapplied, drinks filled and emptied, cars arriving and departing, pavement crossed, miles traveled, the purse in hand. She was beautiful, she was reckless, she was lost, she was aging. She was unstoppable, too, because there's power in pain, even when we don't know it.

I witnessed this woman transform from someone who looked outward to someone who looked within. She had moments, like all of us, long moments looking in the mirror at her changing visage. At other times, she fixed her stare across the city, longing for something without; it's almost palpable in some of the images, this longing. But there's a pivotal moment in the book where she turns and looks right at me. It's startling. It's everything. I knew then, when I see her at rest with her new partner, that not only did her gaze take me out across the sea, she, too, went there and came back at last.

— Ann Jastrab

Biographies

JACQUE RUPP

Jacque Rupp is a documentary and fine-art photographer based in the San Francisco Bay Area. A visual storyteller, Rupp uses the camera to challenge and question, offering a unique perspective on the world around us. In her most recent work, Rupp focuses on womanhood, using herself and her experiences. As the subject matter, Rupp ventures off into the imagined, exploring issues of identity and purpose.

Rupp received an MBA from Santa Clara University and later worked as an executive in Silicon Valley. Building on her lifelong passion for the visual arts, Rupp studied photography at Stanford University, at the Los Angeles Center of Photography, and at Santa Fe Workshops. She is on the advisory board for the UNAFF (United Nations Associated Film Festival) and serves on the board of the Weston Collective, a nonprofit organization dedicated to expanding student access to photography.

Her photographs are held in private collections and have been exhibited widely in juried shows and publications. Rupp's documentary work on farmers in the Salinas Valley has been used by numerous nonprofit organizations both in print and online. Jacque Rupp was selected as a Critical Mass finalist in 2022 and 2023.

ELINOR CARUCCI

Fine-art photographer Elinor Carucci was born in Jerusalem in 1971. Her work has been included in many solo and group exhibitions worldwide and appeared in publications internationally. Her work is in the collections of MoMA, the Jewish Museum, the Brooklyn Museum, and many others.

She was awarded the ICP Infinity Award in 2001, a Guggenheim Fellowship in 2002, and an NYFA Fellowship in 2010. Carucci has published four monographs to date: *Closer*, *Diary of a Dancer*, *MOTHER*, *Midlife*, and most recently, *The Collars of Ruth Bader Ginsburg*.

Carucci currently teaches at the graduate programs of photography at School of Visual Arts and is represented by Edwynn Houk Gallery.

JASON LANGER

Jason Langer's photography is known for its sense of mystery, eroticism, and suspense. His work is rooted in universal mystical ideas, his Jewish upbringing, and Buddhist and Jungian concepts. He has published four monographs distributed worldwide, including *Secret City* (Nazraeli Press, 2006), *Possession* (Nazraeli Press, 2013), the midcareer retrospective *Twenty Years* (Radius Books, 2015) and *Berlin* (Kerber Verlag, 2022). Supported by grants from the Ford Family Foundation, the Joy of Giving Something Foundation, the Oregon Arts Commission, and the Wood Institute, Langer's photographs are held in the permanent collections of Jordan Schnitzer Museum of Art, Yale University Art Gallery, Zimmerli Art Museum, Sir Elton John, Sir Mick Jagger, and the International Photography Hall of Fame and Museum, and are represented or distributed by CLAMP (New York), Galerie Esther Woerdehoff (Paris), and Gilman Contemporary (Sun Valley, Idaho). Langer has been published in the *New York Times*, *Vanity Fair*, *American Photographer*, and countless other publications and exhibits, and publishes regularly. Langer lives in Portland, Oregon.

ANN JASTRAB

Ann Jastrab, executive director of the Center for Photographic Art, is a champion of photographic artists. After earning her MFA in photography at the Savannah College of Art and Design in 1995, she joined the resident faculty at the Maine Photographic Workshops and taught there for nearly a decade in both their year-round program and their intensive summer workshops.

Prior to taking the position of executive director of CPA, she curated many exhibitions for RayKo during her tenure as gallery director, while also jurying, curating, and organizing numerous exhibitions for other national and international venues outside of the San Francisco Bay Area. She has served on numerous boards and fundraising committees and has been thrilled to bring her talents, passion, and leadership skills to the Center for Photographic Arts. Besides being a curator and an educator, Ann is a writer and editor, and she is also a fine-art photographer who still carries around a wooden view camera…and a metal one too.

Acknowledgments

And, in no particular order, my sincere gratitude to my many teachers, mentors, friends, and family for making this book possible. I want to thank each and every one of you for your undying support from the bottom of my heart. You have been there for me, for long conversations often late into the night, for photographing, for accompanying me on adventures, and most of all, for believing in me. You have opened your hearts and minds and sometimes even your homes to me. Thank you.

Marsha Guggenheim
Stephen Starkman
Annette LeMay Burke
Chris Scheerder
Lori Ordover
Mamen Saura
Karen Constine
Mark Tuschman
Joji and Hugo Santos
Tatiana Jordan
Michael Itkoff
Ursula Damm
Eric Joseph
Katie Dougherty (Yuschak)
David Rock
Meg Griffiths
Lynn Cianfarani
Joan Haseltine
Sibylle Whittam
Ann Reeves
Jennifer McClure
Maggie Steber
Elinor Carucci
Jason Langer
Aline Smithson
Ann Jastrab
Joanne Dugan
Elizabeth Avedon
Carole Simone

And most of all to my loving family: Betty, Edward, Chris, Jordan, Emmy, David, Katie, and DR.